Without A Compass
Charting Course to a Deeper, More Meaningful Life

Shawn Hamill

Copyright © 2024

All Rights Reserved

Dedication

I dedicate this book to my wife Leanne, and son Daeyten both of whom accompanied me on my journey from the corporate jungle to spiritual freedom. They inspire me every day to live life free of limitations. I also dedicate it to my late father who I thank for instilling his values in me, while always encouraging me to follow my dreams... I miss you every day!!

One final mention goes out to every person who has heard our story and whispered "one day" ... I encourage you to make today that day!

Table of Contents

CHAPTER 1 – ROUGH SEAS TO PARADISE 5
    The Three Personas 11
CHAPTER 2 - AGAINST THE GRAIN 17
    Lost Not At Sea 19
CHAPTER 3 – FINDING BALANCE 25
    The Three Pillars of a Balanced Life 28
CHAPTER 4 – FILLING YOUR BUCKET 38
    The Six Fundamentals of Fulfilment 43
CHAPTER 5 - THE WIND THAT FILLS YOUR SAIL 56
    It's On You 60
    The Enemy Within 62
    For Whom the Change Tolls 64
CHAPTER 6 - DREAMLESS SEAS 69
    Beware of Limiting Beliefs 74
    The Fear Factor 75
    Let Fear Work for You 79
    Daring To Dream 101 80
    Power Of Perseverance 86
CHAPTER 7 - UNTANGLE YOUR ANCHOR 91
    Get Off the Rumble Strip 92
    Learned Helplessness 94
    Clear Your Head of Clutter 99
CHAPTER 8 - SELLING YOUR VISION 105

Building Bridges 108
Whose Idea Was This? 110
Role Play 113

CHAPTER 9 - MAP TO THE SIMPLE LIFE 119

Dead Reckoning…Determine Your True Position 123
Where Do You Want to Be? 126

CHAPTER 10 - SEE BEYOND THE HORIZON 130

Eight Habits of a Visionary 135

CHAPTER 11 - CHART CONVICTION 147

Goal Setting Roadblocks 149

CHAPTER 12 – STAY THE COURSE 153

Maintain The Rhumb Line 157
See It from Your Team's Eyes 160
Know The Pitfalls 161
Think Outside the Triangle 162
Dead Reckoning 163
Live Your Story 164

CHAPTER 13 - STEPPING STONES TO YOUR BEST LIFE 168

Eight Rules For A Better Life 173

CHAPTER 14 – BUILDING YOUR COMMUNITY 180

The Power of a Smile 181
The Power of a Name 182
Show Interest/Be Curious 184
Acknowledgement 185

CHAPTER 15 - THE POWER OF YOUR FIRST STEP 187

    Psychological Momentum 189

    If At First You Don't Succeed….. 190

    The WWIP Method.. 191

CHAPTER 16: TAME THE STRESS MONSTER 196

    Burnout is Real… and Dangerous 196

    The Three Pillars Guide to a Balanced Life 201

CHAPTER 17 - TIME TO NAVIGATE.. 212

    The Domino Effect 215

    Eyes On the Journey 216

    Trust Your Inner Compass... 220

CHAPTER 18 - COLLATERAL BEAUTY 222

EPILOGUE 229

    Closing the Loop 229

    Where Are We Now?... 235

    Acknowledgements.. 236

CHAPTER 1 – ROUGH SEAS TO PARADISE

"What separates people capable of greatness from those who've achieved greatness is the ability to overcome their fear of taking a chance." ~ Shawn Hamill

The plane had just reached cruising altitude at around 30,000 feet. It was my 8th flight in two weeks and my 70th flight of the year. I had logged more than 90 hotel nights. But my focus was elsewhere. I began to ponder what it would be like - jumping from a perfectly functional plane, for no better reason than "because I can." It was the moment I realized I was stuck, and I was looking for a way to break free.

I have two great fears in my life: heights and deep water. Here I was flying over Lake Ontario, contemplating a thought as scary as I could imagine. Yet I could not escape the curiosity of the moment. I silently asked myself why people obsess with jumping out of airplanes. Why do they choose to give up relative safety in submitting themselves to forces beyond their control? Even though the mere thought made me enormously uncomfortable, I could not shift my attention.

Ironically, I was at a similar crossroads in my career. The time was quickly approaching where I would be forced to make a decision. I had a good job with significant responsibility. I was managing a sales division in a region that included all of Canada and the eastern USA. I had won the Chairman's Club Award of Sales Excellence two years in a row for being the leader of the top-producing sales team. I was on my way to our head office in Bradenton, Florida, where I expected I would be awarded it for a third consecutive year. My focus, however, was inescapably locked on a thought that was terrorizing me while intriguing me at the same time.

Organizational changes were looming. My team and I had been shifted from the Consumer division to the Industrial division, and it seemed to be an awkward fit. My customers were home improvement retailers who sell to contractors, and consumers. The industrial realm was all about selling volume to Original Equipment Manufacturer (OEM) accounts. OEM customers buy product in bulk, re-brand it, and market it under their own brand. My world was about selling branded value add - not commodities.

The company hired a new leader to the role of Vice President (VP), to head up the division. The new guy was an intellect with a PhD in Building Sciences and a reputation for having absolutely no modesty. If there was credit to be given, the word was, he would always find a way to land it solely on his own shoulders.

Two months earlier, our first opportunity to work together was at a negotiation with an industry buying group. It was an annual ritual that I had become quite familiar with. The meeting went excellent until the new guy started talking. Suddenly, the done deal was undone, and he gave 5% away before we re-did it. As we walked away, he bragged about how he saved the deal that was never in jeopardy. It didn't take long before he started into me with the typical bluster of an insecure micro-manager. "There are going to be changes," and "Things will be done my way," he bellowed.

Almost instantly, I asked myself, *Do I really need this?* The follow-up question that bounced around the confines of my simple mind was, *Will it be different anywhere else?*

Nonetheless, I put my name out to some industry contacts and soon had a few options to consider. Each had its own pros and cons, but the one that stood out was a US building products manufacturer that had no Canadian treasury. In other words, they had no Canadian employees and no familiarity with Canadian employment laws. However, they needed someone to manage and grow their Canadian business. I was introduced to them by a customer of mine and was intrigued by the growth potential I envisioned.

After a few months of back-and-forth discussion, we concluded the best option was for them to hire me as a contracted commissioned agent for all of Canada. What appealed to me was the independence that this opportunity would grant. I would have the freedom I was seeking: freedom from micro-management and freedom to do other things. I could venture into other products to represent, could set my own schedule, and outline my own priorities. I would have the freedom to focus on things that were important to me.

On the cons side, one thing stood out: I would be independent. No salary, no benefits, and no one waiting in the wings to pay back the expenses I incurred.

I would start my own business, build my own team, and my income would be based entirely upon what was sold into the Canadian market. All expenses would come from my pocket. I wouldn't have a parachute.

Just before the meeting in Florida that I was travelling to, the new VP was questioned about a decision he made, authorizing the hire of new contract sales members. We had discussed the plan in detail, and he agreed to it with a clear set of expectations. Rather than defend the decision he made, he chose to accuse me of insubordination in an email strand that included several senior members of the organization. My first response was to offer an olive branch by suggesting that perhaps I misunderstood his instruction. I felt it served me no purpose to call out this person and threaten his ego.

Rather than accept the olive branch, he doubled down by becoming more aggressive arguing there was no mistake and asserting that I intentionally chose to defy him. Feeling cornered, he left me no option but to defend myself with the facts. I replied with proof that he was the one who was mistaken in the form of an email he sent to me authorizing the plan that we discussed.

While the plane hurdled through the air at more than 500 MPH, my distaste for the new VP, and his betrayal had me asking myself if that was enough to justify giving up the relative safety I enjoyed in my current role. It led me to wonder what other reasons were causing me to consider the seemingly risky opportunity that was presented to me.

A bad boss? The fear that I had plateaued in my current role? None of these things seemed significant enough to jump without a parachute. It gave me pause to reflect on my situation.

I started this new division for the Canadian market. In three years, I grew the program's sales from $300,000 to $7M per year. This was despite selling against a competitor that was a brand giant. When our US division struggled to get traction, I was tapped to add it to my responsibilities. In six months, I was poised to turn things around and make serious inroads. It felt like this was my baby. The new reality I faced in this moment was an absolute unexpected gut punch.

The new VP made me realize that things change, and generally, there is only a limited amount of change within your control. What became obvious was it was time for me to focus my energy on that which I could control. I resolved that change had to come - the opportunity to start my own business and build my own team seemed to be the kind of change I was looking for, but something still seemed to be missing.

In the role I was in, I was making good money. I had a financial plan and was well on my way to building a retirement savings nest egg. By all accounts, I was on track or better. But something told me that this new opportunity, or any new opportunity on its own, wasn't going to make everything perfect again.

Something was out of balance.

The Three Personas

In my search for what was missing, some things started to come into focus. Within us all, it's generally agreed that we have opposing forces that influence every decision we make. I call these forces my 3 personas, and while you might have your own names for them, I've named them *Dreamer Self, Responsible Self and Headshaker.*

The Dreamer Self - Throughout our history, many inspirational people have challenged expectations and went on to achieve great things. Their commonality is their unwillingness to accept the norms and expectations of society.

Growing up, I was one of those people. I refused to accept that my sole purpose in life was to go to school, get a degree, then use it in a 9-5 existence for the next 30-40 years in hopes of an exciting retirement that would last more than a blink of an eye. That is my Dreamer Self persona. I call him Dreamer Shawn.

Dreamer Shawn pledged at a young age that I would sell t-shirts on the beach when I grew up. It wasn't so much that I was a budding entrepreneur. I simply loved the ocean, the beach, and the romantic vision of freedom and tranquility that they presented to me.

I've always found it to be magical how sea air and warm sand could melt away any stress or anxiety I was feeling in a moment. Staring out to the sea is like a catalyst, daring me to dream. I dreamed of faraway lands and wondered what it was like for early explorers to ship off from a safe port, challenging the unknown, for no other reason than because they can… or must.

The sea could always draw me in. Yet, its vast unknown was also dark and scary. Just as I understood the sea could be tranquil and peaceful, I also knew it could turn on you. The sea can quickly become an unrelenting beast capable of pulling you into its clutches and not letting go. As a person who likes to be in control, the sea terrifies me every bit as much as it romances me.

While all of us have some element of a Dreamer Self persona, how dominant it is varies from person to person. Its level of dominance even varies within us through different stages of our lives.

The Responsible Self - Being born into and raised in a traditional middle-class family, my father struggled to understand me. He was a businessman who taught me that honesty, integrity, and hard work were the principles that made a man. In my view, he succeeded at pretty much any task he pursued. His world wasn't about dreams. His world was about the value of a hard day's work. He was the epitome of the theory that you're born, you go to school, you get a diploma/degree, then you work hard until you retire - 9-5 to 65. The ability to put dinner on the table was his measurement of success. My vision of selling t-shirts on the beach drove him crazy! Perhaps that was my goal.

My father was the classic definition of the dominate Responsible Self persona. The Responsible Self persona is determined to steer us through life on a safe course. Its goal is to see us make good decisions that will lead us on a life that feeds our necessities. For the Responsible Self, life is about being practical. Dreams, in its view, are not practical. Dreams don't pay the bills.

Responsible self is critical to your existence even in your formative years. This persona is what disciplines you to learn and develop the necessary skills to exist in society. The difficulty is that it's easy for our Responsible Self persona to become dominant, leaving no space for Dreamer Self to grow and gain influence. As a result, by the time we reach adulthood, it's common that the Responsible Self is well-entrenched as the dominant persona, controlling all major decisions in our lives.

We all need to have a presence of the Responsible Self persona in our lives, but we must be sure to manage and restrain its influence if we wish to discover purpose and fulfilment in our lives.

The vision required to realize remarkable feats lives in the mindset of the Dreamer Self Persona, but the Responsible Self persona brings an element of practicality to the process when they collaborate.

As a young adult, I actively began to question if there was more to life than 9-5 to 65 that my Responsible Self had become so active in promoting. My Dreamer Self never truly stopped wondering if there was a shortcut or a backdoor to some sort of alternate reality where I could become what I was truly meant to be?

Responsible Shawn would rationalize there was no shame in becoming who my dad had become. He was an honorable man and a provider who was respected by many. Dreamer Shawn would question whether that alone would be a life truly lived?

The Headshaker Self - The reality was that my Responsible Self and Dreamer Self personas both existed in my life, but they had not yet learned how to compromise and collaborate with each other.

When these two personas fail to collaborate, it creates a perfect opportunity for the 3rd persona to become dominant. This is the Headshaker Self. The Headshaker persona should never be given the opportunity to become influential in your life. It thrives in the role of eternal pessimist. The Headshaker wants you to exist in a world of can't, won't, and never will. When your Responsible Self and Dreamer Self personas refuse or are unable to collaborate, you can count on the Headshaker Self persona to swoop in with an "I told you so" mindset with the goal of convincing you that nothing remarkable will ever be possible.

The purpose of having a Headshaker persona should be to challenge you to use critical thinking as an important part of your decision-making process. That said, critical thinking should be a give-and-take between Responsible Self and Dreamer Self. Any input from the Headshaker should only be considered in terms of making sure your decision has considered all REASONABLE threats to the decision you've come to.

Compass Point Reflections:

1) The Three Personas – Dreamer Self, Responsible Self, and Headshaker.
2) Ask yourself which personas exist in your life, and which dominate your decisions. Why?
3) Consider what, if any, change is needed.

"Alone we can do so little; together we can do so much."

- Helen Keller"

CHAPTER 2 - AGAINST THE GRAIN

"When everything seems to be going against you, remember that the airplane takes off against the wind, not with it." ~ Henry Ford

The human race progressed from the stone age because there were always those who chose to go against the grain. In a time when some argued the world was flat, Christopher Columbus challenged that narrative in search for a new route to India. Since then, many aspects of our lives are what they are today merely because someone successfully challenged popular wisdom and developed a better way.

In my own life, I blessed my father for giving me such strong and principled guidance, I was never one to learn without questioning. On the surface, it drove my father crazy, but I felt he had a secret admiration for my willingness to always challenge the popular narrative. I loved him dearly for accepting me for who I was. He was a strait-laced, conservative man who could still joke that "Shawn marches to his own beat."

By 18, my independent spirit was on full display. I would make it regular practice to challenge my father's ideology merely because I was 18. It would drive most fathers nuts, but usually my father would make a comment, smile, and change the subject.

By that time, the one thing we had in common, more than anything else, was a love for boats. It was around this time, that he brought home a 30' boat that he purchased in Quebec while on a business trip.

While he was fiercely proud of his purchase, the rest of the family, and most friends, shuddered at the sight of this "project" that he had brought home. Clearly, in an advanced stage of dilapidation, this "vessel" had holes on the deck and throughout the hull. The stern (back of the boat) was barely holding on. It lacked an engine and most of the vital components required to be operational. Nonetheless, my dad had a vision. It was a vision that he saw through over the span of 18 months that required a rebuild of almost the entire boat. As he prepared to launch, he pondered with me about what he should name his pride and joy. I suggested "Silent Chuckle" in reference to all those who joked that the only part of a lake it would ever see was the bottom.

My father instantly adopted *Silent Chuckle* and launched her a short while later. I watched, breathlessly, wondering if all his blood, sweat, and tears were enough to make her seaworthy. Luckily it was, and he enjoyed several seasons with her. For me, it was a remarkable discovery to realize that my father had a Dreamer Self persona, alive and well, that saw to the successful re-birth, and launch of *Silent Chuckle*!

As his dream became reality, and his love for *Silent Chuckle* solidified, I took over another boat that he had purchased for me and my brother when I was 8 years old. It was a 12' *Sea Snark* day sailor that he got from K-Mart. Made of styrofoam, with no motor, I learned to use the sails to work around small inland lakes whenever I could find the time. This was the beginning of my sailing dream.

Lost Not At Sea

By then, my rebellious spirit was beginning to give way to the principles of hard work that pops instilled in me. I worked part time from grade 10 through my college years and held down a full-time job during the summer. When I finished college and began to consider the possibility of growing up, I got spooked. Until then, I had convinced myself that my destiny was living a simple life, such as I mentioned before - selling t-shirts on the beach. Suddenly this growing up concept was present and seemed dangerous. The rational response I came up with late on a

Saturday night was to head west, accepting a job as a front desk clerk at a resort in Lake Louise, AB. I experienced some fun days, but about a week in, I was back on a bus headed back east, and three days later, I arrived back in Toronto.

Six months later, I found myself engaged and only months away from becoming a father. Responsible Self was suddenly living large in my life! It seemed like growing up had become inevitable.

Jumping forward to the moment I was sitting on the Florida-bound plane to go meet with the new VP, I wondered how I ever became such a Responsible Self? Was it the failed trip out west that altered my course and led me to become a person I respected but couldn't identify with through the eyes of my Dreamer Self?

Dreamer Shawn still held onto the memory of that younger Shawn who left his family home and went on the adventure west. Dreamer Shawn was thankful for that experience, rather than fearful of the fact it didn't turn out exactly as planned. The moment made me realize I was only feeding Responsible Shawn. I had lost touch with Dreamer Shawn and what his needs were.

I knew then that my life had become one-dimensional. I was focussed on my career and little else. If I stayed on that path, I would continue to drift further away from my family and anything else that was truly important to me. My true self was lost.

Unfortunately, this is a stark reality that becomes life for most people. We dream wild dreams as youth, but society conditions us to believe that dreams are meant to be just that… dreams. I remember telling my high school guidance counsellor that I wanted to work in professional sports when I grew up. Rather than detail the many ways a talentless athlete could still become employed in pro sports, he replied "is there anything else you're interested in?"

Most of us get streamed into an almost pre-determined role in society that typically comes as a result of happenstance or environmental conditions that surround us. That was me as I hurdled through the air, headed to Florida. I practically fell into the place I was in life from a combination of happenstance and environmental circumstances. I became a father before I had prepared myself fully for the role and ended up in sales largely because it followed in the footsteps of my father. He was good at sales, so I strived to be better.

Life was far from terrible. I had a house, kids, a beautiful wife, and we managed to find a way to spend a couple of weeks per year living the dream life on a beach sipping on mojitos. What more could I ask for, right? Why would I ever go against the grain, and leave all this behind?

The corporate world is full of people like that. As they graduate college, unsure of what's next, they take a role that is supposed to be temporary until they decide what they want to be when they grow up. As they learn the role they become good at it. When they become good at it, they develop the 2 C's, Confidence and Comfort. Soon they become the seniors in the role that others look up to. This leads to more confidence and more comfort. Then they're offered a promotion, which they accept, gaining more confidence and comfort. Eventually we get to a point where we've defined ourselves, our entire identity, by the title on our business card and the description of the role. We convince ourselves that that is who we are and what we were always meant to do.

There is absolutely nothing wrong with that as long as you have not left a significant part of you behind. But sometimes the role you've chosen to identify yourself by really is the temporary one you said it was when you first started, yet you refuse to acknowledge it. You rationalize that things are good, so where is the harm in just going with the grain? Perhaps you're 40 or 45 - or whatever age you consider is too old to re-define yourself. Or maybe you just got so absorbed in the life you came to accept that you missed the sign that was indicative of the opportunity to re-invent yourself. Whatever the case may be, going against the grain and setting a plan in motion to become who you truly desire to become won't seem easy. Making it easy starts with determination. Starting the process of change begins with committing to change. Committing to go against what society teaches us is the practical choice and accepting that giving into Dreamer Self is a viable alternative. We are conditioned to believe that Dreamer Self can't feed us, clothe us or give us shelter. Dare to consider whether Dreamer Self is the source of all energy required to achieve this and so much more from life.

Compass Point Reflections:

1) Rate yourself 1-10 - 1 being a person who always goes with the grain, and 10 being always goes against the grain. Where are you now, and where do you aspire to be? Are You Lost or Found?

2) Take a few minutes to define yourself.
   a) Does the definition come easily, or do you struggle?

b) Does your definition align with both your Dreamer Self, and Responsible Self?
c) How often does Headshaker Self get to have a voice?

"The best sermons are lived, not preached"

~ Anonymous

CHAPTER 3 – FINDING BALANCE

"Most of us spend too much time on what is urgent and not enough time on what is important." ~ Stephen Covey, Author of *The 7 Habits of Highly Effective People*

As my flight hurdled south toward Florida, I took inventory of where I was in life. I had two kids with the youngest due to graduate high school in a year. I was newly married to Leanne, my second wife. We had a home and a solid life. It wasn't the dream of selling t-shirts on the beach, but it was a solid life all its own. It was SAFE. Perhaps I had I become my father?

I felt I was in a state of non-living. Until then, I was climbing the corporate ladder, and making a name for myself. I had changed roles every 4-5 years, allowing for rapid advancement. Each new opportunity brought a new challenge, more responsibility, and greater reward. I answered the bell with each new opportunity, yet when the workday was over, I felt empty. It seemed like the only identity I had was the title on my business card. When people asked what I did, I referred them to that title. When they asked what I did outside of work, I drew a blank. Drinking wine with my wife while enjoying a nice dinner hardly seemed like a full and balanced life.

I got so busy living in the now, so busy defining my career, that I lost sight of my whole identity.

Not long after the plane entered Florida airspace, the Gulf of Mexico was in sight. As we approached Tampa Bay, we were put into a holding pattern. Circling above the gulf, I noticed a fleet of sailboats floating in harmony on the water. I contemplated the freedom that would come from living life on the water just like that. Moving into a "neighborhood" and dropping anchor. When you became tired of your surroundings, it would be as simple as pulling anchor.

This brought me back to a time when Dreamer Shawn was highly active in my life. I reflected on many a Saturday, on many a lake, where I spent the day sailing in my little Sea Snark. I would hit the lake early in the morning and often stay out till dusk. It was about more than sailing. It was about the freedom of being on the water, riding the wind. I used to dream of a lifestyle…exactly the lifestyle I was seeing through that plane window… Freedom, living by the sea, and the ability to move on to endless destinations worldwide.

I came to realize that memories that were stirring in me were memories of when I enjoyed a much more balanced life.

What I had discovered was that I had taken "growing up" too far. Becoming a father was something that happened to me before I had planned for it. That meant I had not taken the to time to discover how to become a father, or a balanced adult for that matter. I obsessed with becoming what I saw as a role model. My father was a successful, driven businessman who never let me down. Despite any struggles he and my mother might have encountered, what I saw was a table that always had food and a home that kept us warm and dry.

I became consumed in my career to provide these same things to my family. I made my career my entire identity.

In that moment, I realized that either I had completely forgotten what a balanced life was, or I had just given up on the pursuit of the same. The emptiness that gnawed at me told me that changes were needed before burn out consumed me and undermined all hope of finding balance and purpose.

I began detailing what I needed back in my life.

- I needed more freedom to serve more than just my career;
- I needed to keep my promise to live the life I had envisioned;
- I needed to rediscover the passion that inspired me many years ago; and
- I needed to stop living on autopilot and become accountable to self, in my pursuit of a life of fulfilment.

In my notebook, I started to chisel out "The Three Pillars of a Balanced Life," a set of guidelines that I would use to guide me back from chaos to a life of balance.

The Three Pillars of a Balanced Life

It is said that a pyramid is the most solid shape that you can use in construction. In ancient times, Egyptians adopted this philosophy to develop pyramids that have lasted thousands of years. In more modern times, tripods are used to stabilize many things from cameras to construction instruments.

In life, we can also use this shape to understand what is required to live a balanced life. I call this The Three Pillars of a Balanced Life.

Self Pillar - Sadly, many people of my generation generally tend to spend the least amount of time focussed on Self. Rarely do we ever view attention to Self with the same urgency as the other two pillars. In fact, our influence comes from previous generations, who survived some or all of two world wars, the depression, and post war/depression austerity. They were conditioned to believe it was selfish to put our own needs ahead of others.

By contrast younger generations seem to be more in tune with serving their Self pillar. Some question whether it is at the expense of the community or career pillars at times. From generation to generation there are shifting mindsets. Time will perhaps tell us which blend of perspective is most ideal. What is of most importance is that we understand that a healthy Self pillar is the cornerstone of the solid foundation of character needed to support the load of the three pillars of balance.

Think of your Self pillar as the foundation from which you will serve the other two pillars. If your Self pillar isn't as strong as granite, it will crumble under the pressure that your career and family/community pillars will exert.

In 1989, Author David Chilton wrote a fictional account about personal finances. The concept he wrote about was dubbed "Pay yourself first". The lead Character, Roy, offers financial advice to customers in his barbershop. The idea is that one should set aside and invest 10% of income for savings, before using your income for anything else - hence the concept of "pay yourself first". If you continue to build this up, it will ensure you have the resources for a healthy retirement. *The Wealthy Barber* has sold over 5 million copies and inspired many to build a life of prosperity.

Making Self your primary priority in life works in a similar way. To be effective in our careers, or in our family lives, we must not only show up. We must show up energized, and ready to face the challenges ahead. That means taking the time to serve yourself.

A good meal and a good night's sleep will give you the physical energy to challenge the rigors of your day. What will feed your soul, and give you the mental energy to truly show up and be present?

Right now, think of three things that energize you. Is it exercise, meditation, a massage, or something else? Write them down, then ask yourself: Do you regularly commit to these things before all else to replenish yourself?

If you struggle to regularly serve your personal well-being, challenge yourself to change that. To start, define a minimum of two healthy things that can energize you. Common activities include:

1) Meditation
2) Exercise
3) Walking or Hiking
4) Sitting by the Water
5) Stretching
6) Eating Healthy
7) Yoga
8) A Power Nap
9) Journalling
10) Reading
11) Experiencing Nature
12) Twenty Minutes Unplugged

For an entire month commit to finding the time to complete those two tasks for at least 10 - 30 minutes daily.

Each day actively observe how much energy you bring to the other two pillars of your life as a result of serving yourself first.

Once you get into the habit of doing this, and see the positive results it creates, you will appreciate how creating a healthier Self pillar can improve all aspects of your life. Use that as justification to remain committed to serving your Self pillar first.

Family and Community Pillar - Family includes many people. The most obvious are those who bring us into this world: our parents and their parents. Of course, we include our children and siblings into this cohort as well. Then there are our friends - the family that we get to choose.

As you establish yourself in your career, you will likely even include some colleagues and co-workers into the network that you call family or community.

No matter the relationship, this network of people in your life will become valuable in countless ways. They will serve you when you need support, and you will feed your soul when the opportunity presents to serve them.

Sadly, we often tend to underserve this pillar in busy times. Ask yourself how many times you've missed a family or friend event because you were too busy at work?

Naturally you can't always be in all places at all times. The demands of a busy career can be inflexible. To strengthen your community pillar, you need commit to make up times. For example, when you miss a soccer game due to a business trip, be sure to schedule time to make up for that. When you can't make it to a friend's birthday, ask if you can meet for lunch at a time convenient to both. At all times, ask yourself if that work project really can't wait when the family commitments warrant it. If an employer can't understand your commitment to each of the three pillars of a balanced life, explain how you are serving their needs by making yourself stronger. If they still can't comprehend, perhaps you might consider if other options might suit your life better.

Career Pillar - What often occurs as we enter adulthood is that we focus on our careers first once we finish our education and enter the working world. We dive deep into defining ourselves, and trying to capture the attention of those who can be impactful to our career development.

Through our successes and our failures, we begin to shape meaningful values that we will carry with us through the rest of our lives. Far too often, however, we can become absorbed in developing our identity through what we do in our career. Ask yourself the question, "What do you do?". Is your response monopolized by your career? Or is your natural response multi-dimensional, describing you in your entirety?

There is no shame in being proud of what you do for a living and allowing it to become a major part of your identity, but there needs to be a balance among all three pillars. Studies show that a lack of balance can cause you to lose focus, become disengaged, and it is a leading cause of burnout.

Before I discovered the concept of the Three Pillars of a Balanced Life, I felt trapped. My career was good, and it helped us to afford luxuries that we enjoyed. The lack of balance left me with many questions or concerns. It seemed that the more success I achieved the further away I got from the life I once envisioned, and the things I valued most. At the same time, that success was starting to feel a bit like a runaway train that I could not slow down.

Having acknowledged my feeling of being trapped was a low point for me, in a sense, but it was also the wake-up call that helped me realize how important a balanced life is. Once I defined the principles of the *Three Pillars of a Balanced Life*, I was able to look critically at my life through the lens of each pillar and detail what was good and what was missing in each pillar.

What I discovered is that I was not serving my Self pillar well at all. While I was serving the Family pillar, it was without a regular commitment and only when my Career pillar allowed it. I would come home from a long business trip and check emails well into the evening and on weekends after I had failed to serve my family and self for several days.

Responsible Shawn was large and in charge in my life and was almost entirely focused on serving the Career pillar of my life. Dreamer Shawn was on life support, and the Family and Self pillars were suffering as a result. This gave my Headshaker persona the opportunity to move in and become firmly entrenched. This caused me to fall into a spiral of negative thoughts - a trap where I convinced myself that if good happened, it was simply a precursor for something bad yet to come. If I got a bonus, I would wait for the car to break down or the roof to start leaking. These were all rumblings of the Headshaker, given a voice due to Dreamer Shawn's lack thereof.

I knew I had to break this thought process and become the instigator of change in my life. I needed to get my Responsible and Dreamer personas to begin collaboration on my path to a more meaningful life and silence the Headshaker.

It's often said that everything happens for a reason. If there is any truth to that, seeing the sailing community from my plane window served to wake me up from my slumber in order to start dreaming again. Fortunately, I had my eyes open and my mind clear enough to see and hear the message. As you work to develop and pursue your dream life, be sure to also have open eyes and an open mind, ensuring you don't miss the message that is meant for you.

Compass Point Reflections

1) Serve Your Self

Find activities that serve your Self pillar physically, spiritually, and holistically, and commit to making them a regular part of your daily routine.

2) Commit To Make Up Times

Life will get in the way of honoring every commitment you have in all three pillars of your balanced life. Set aside time and energy to make up for the commitments that you miss.

3) Ask yourself the question, "What Do I Do?"

If your natural answer to this question lacks balance and is heavily skewed to only one or two of the three pillars, outline a plan to bring back balance.

"The bad news is time flies. The good news is you're the pilot." ~ Michael Altshuler, businessman

CHAPTER 4 – FILLING YOUR BUCKET

"It is not in the pursuit of happiness that we find fulfillment, it is in the happiness of pursuit." ~ Denis Waitley

As I was in the holding pattern over Tampa Bay, the images of the sailing community so far below imprinted on my consciousness. As I began churning up a vision to go sailing, I wondered what would Responsible Self say? What would my wife say? Would the idea serve as yet another way to drive my father crazy? I knew it was an irrational idea in the eyes of many - but not to me. In that moment, it seemed like a lifeline. Instantly, I went from an overwhelming sense of STUCK to suddenly being invigorated by the prospect of freedom. I felt like I now had purpose, even though I had yet to explore exactly what purpose truly is.

Responsible Shawn cautioned me about making a hasty decision without proper planning. The Headshaker laughed and worked hard to convince me I was being ridiculous.

In moments like this, it is important to maintain momentum without getting impatient. Impatience can destroy an exciting idea just as easily as pessimism can.

Once you create your vision, it's okay to allow your Responsible Self to have a say on the idea and be a part of the planning process. Dreamer Self isn't conditioned to worry about details like Responsible Self is. This is why collaboration is so important. You will count on Dreamer Self to keep the energy and determination up, and the best way to do that is to develop a plan to realize your vision that will satisfy both Dreamer Self and Responsible Self. That will silence the Headshaker and pave the way to move forward.

As we made our final approach to Tampa, my mind began to ponder the idea of buying a boat and becoming "liveaboards". As I considered what resources we would need, it occurred to me that I could not answer that question until I had a clearer picture of what such a life would look like. The 25,000 feet above sea level view wasn't a very clear image. More importantly, I realized I could never sell Leanne on such a big change until I could articulate the idea in detail. (She is half Dutch and worked in accounting. Being pragmatic comes naturally to her.)

Upon leaving the airport, I headed straight to the coast looking for marinas, so that I could complete the picture I had drawn up. I took photos, and wandered around several marinas, attempting to capture the vibe of this lifestyle. The one thing that is almost universal to cruising is that where there are boats, you can almost always find restaurants and bars. So, I was able to stake out the marinas without seeming like a stalker. Quicky, I compiled the evidence that I could present to my wife to help her see my vision. Eventually, I arrived at my hotel with a much clearer picture of what my vision was. I wanted to go sailing. More than that, I wanted to live on the water. I wanted to go to sleep to the sound of water lapping on the side of the boat and wake up to breakfast served above deck with a view of the sea. I wanted to not only escape winter but escape the mundane routine of living on land and chase the simplicity and freedom that had escaped me for so long.

That first night in Florida was a restless one for me. It wasn't uncommon for me to struggle to sleep on the first night of a business trip. On this night, I continued to debate the viability of packing up and going sailing. Responsible Shawn and Dreamer Shawn had a lot to offer. What kept coming back to me was "Purpose and Fulfilment". These were things I had now concluded were missing from my life.

As I reflected on the bigger picture of my life, it seemed very much like it was in black and white. I had gone to school, got a good job, started a family, had the house (and the mortgage to prove it), just as I was conditioned to do.

Though I was clicking all the boxes, it was clear that my picture lacked color. I didn't know if pursuing the dream of sailing would bring that color, but I was certain that staying the same course would not. I was acutely aware that I wasn't guaranteed the time and health to follow this dream if I waited until retirement.

What was quickly becoming obvious was that I got so busy at being busy, I hadn't taken the time to figure out what I was so busy for. Sure, being successful is important. It helps pay the bills and gives us reason to take pride in ourselves. But I was starting to grasp the concept of fulfillment, and in that, I was realizing that fulfillment consists of much more than just paying the bills and having pride in what you've accomplished in your career.

A life of fulfillment is ultimately what we all aspire for. Many different labels are used, but "fulfillment" is what best describes our reason for not only showing up in life but for enduring all life can throw at us and continuing on. Before I even boarded that flight to Florida, it was obvious to me that I had yet to discover many of the ingredients of fulfillment.

Now, here I was, dreaming of packing up our lives, selling everything, and going sailing. I had defined what I was looking for - freedom. But ultimately, I had to dig deeper. I had to find meaning that was bigger than me. I had to find something that was universal.

I knew that my wife Leanne was also restless in her career. But, to the best of my awareness, she didn't grow up dreaming of going sailing or selling t-shirts on the beach. When she graduated from high school and got a part-time job at the YMCA, it was to keep busy and put gas in her car until she figured out what she wanted to be when she grew up.

Twenty-seven years later, she was Director of Accounting Services and a volunteer group fitness trainer. She had made many lasting friendships there and enjoyed the volunteer work. But her accounting role was something she fell into. She never considered it her life's work. She was comfortable but not fulfilled.

So, what became universal was that we were both seeking fulfilment. This led me on a quest to define what fulfilment is and learn how to find it. In that journey, I discovered that while fulfillment consists of many ingredients, there are six fundamentals.

The Six Fundamentals of Fulfilment

Make A Passion Statement - Passion is like a super charger. Imagine you are having a challenging day. Add in that you didn't get a great sleep the night before, and you're encountering stress at work. Then envision it's time to complete a task or activity you're passionate about.

Suddenly, your mood and energy can completely change. Even when it's a brief activity like a hike in the woods at lunch hour, you're likely to return to the office invigorated.

Often, we set our passions aside as we begin our careers, and become focused on climbing the corporate ladder, and starting a family.

Rediscovering what you are passionate about is a key step on your road to fulfillment. Take the time to reflect on what you are passionate about or once were.

Ask yourself these questions:

1) What makes you most happy?
2) What are your happiest memories from days gone by?
3) If money wasn't an object, what would you pursue that you aren't pursuing now?
4) When you're having a day of frustration, what activities do you turn to for relaxation?

Look for themes or commonalities in your answers. Don't overthink this. Consider that your first thoughts as you answer each question are likely the most accurate reflection of your true feelings.

As you consciously define the things that you are passionate about write them down as your passion statement and reference them often. Be sure to find ways to serve these passions on a regular basis. Also consider how your passions connect or relate to each of The Three Pillars of a Balanced Life, and include that in your passion statement.

Unleash Your Difference Maker - Now it's time to define your skills and highlight the ones that make you exceptional. List all the skills you practice regularly.

Rank each skill 1 to 10, 10 meaning you are a superstar, and 1 meaning you struggle with that skill. Also take note of whether it is a skill you enjoy or a skill that drains you.

Focus on the skills that are a five or higher, and reflect on each one, while also considering how much enjoyment that skill brings you. Does it serve or starve your passion? The objective is to bring your focus to 1-3 top skills that you enjoy, and will bring you closer to re-discovering your passion. Congratulations – these are your "difference makers."

A key element of the dream life is the opportunity to pursue your passions while using your difference maker in a way that serves the three pillars.

For me, it would have been easy to list selling as a skill that I excel at but instead I dug deeper by listing, and ranking the individual skills that make me good in sales. My top 3 skills, reflective of both my ability and enjoyment, were:

1) Ability to inspire a vision
2) Strategic planning

3) Creative problem solving

The skill that ranked lowest on my list was "attention to detail". In acknowledging this, I also recognized it's a skill that my wife excels in. This meant I needed to become intentional about leaning on her for that skill.

When I started my business, a sales agency, my difference makers were skills that were important for success. That served my career pillar well. Fortunately, each of these skills also served me well in re-discovering my passion for sailing. That served my Self pillar well. I knew that if my wife and son came on board, all 3 pillars would be served.

Acknowledge Your Growth - In all that we do, we always aspire for growth. If you are a hockey player, you strive to score more goals than you did the season previous. Golfers seek to lower their score, while weightlifters seek to increase what they can lift.

In the Oxford Dictionary, fulfillment is defined as "the achievement of something desired, promised, or predicted". Strangely, it doesn't mention anything about sailing - but it also didn't say it CAN'T be about sailing!

Growth is something that we can measure to document our progress towards "the achievement of something desired, promised, or predicted".

The summer before we left to sail south. Leanne and I were sitting on our boat at a dock one evening. A neighbor boat passed by - headed out for the weekend. It was well past dusk, and I remember saying, "I wish we could be confident enough to head out at night rather than always waiting till the morning". That was on a lake, in protected waters, with a short trip ahead. As I tell you our story, we'll see whether or not we realized that growth.

Be sure to park your growth acknowledgements in a safe place in your mind, as they are invaluable for overcoming moments of doubt or frustration and a great way to silence the Headshaker!

In your career, growth can come in the form of increasing sales, getting that promotion, or successfully completing a course that enhances your ability to do your job. For your Self and community pillars, establishing key indicators of growth can be less obvious, but they are equally important. Become intentional about establishing growth indicators relating to all Three pillars of your life.

While it's well known that growth increases your perceived value in the eyes of your work community, documenting progress in any pillar is an excellent way to build your perception of self-worth. In times of adversity, measured growth also serves as great motivation to continue on.

As a sales manager, I encounter two types of responses to the measurement of growth: the rep having a good year loves it when the measurement of growth is applied, while the rep who is having a bad year avoids it at all costs.

Growth should never be used as or considered a bad thing. It is a tool that tells a story. It will tell you how far you've come and how much further you have to go.

In your family pillar growth can come from things you do to become a better parent, spouse, sibling, or friend.

In your Self pillar growth comes from the many ways we improve ourselves, be it physical exercise, reading, meditation, or a litany of other possibilities.

What is most important about growth is to develop a system of measuring and tracking it. As we've discussed already, journalling is an excellent way to track growth. Each day, write in your journal details about how your day was. Make a note of your wins, and detail what you learned from every experience, even when you realize a result that was less than hoped for. Be quantitative, when possible, so that as you review it in later days, you will be able to see the growth you have achieved. This can be a part of the journal I've already suggested you keep as you read this book. Or perhaps keep a separate journal for your ongoing daily journaling.

Seek Your Purpose, Live With Purpose - The Oxford Dictionary defines "purpose" as "the reason for which something is done or created or for which something exists".

Essentially, what Oxford is saying is that purpose is the why, such as WHY you exist, and fulfilment is the WHAT, such as what you experience upon completion of a task. It stops short of connecting the two. Let's do just that.

Too often in life, people search for their purpose in order to determine their course. Instead, I challenge you to let purpose find you.

For many years, I believed that becoming a father would give me purpose. The instant I held my first born in my arms for the first time, it became definite that fatherhood was a part of my purpose. But I also felt that purpose must have other elements to it. Using the Three Pillars of a Well-Balanced Life model, I realized that fatherhood served primarily my Self pillar, even though it impacted all three.

While it took me a while to find my career's purpose, moving into sales was the turning point. For me, a career in sales was about discovering people's problems and providing solutions. I'm good at it, and it stirred a passion within me, thereby serving my Career and Self pillars. The fact that it also furnished me with a good life served my Self and Family pillars.

As my career developed, I was able to realize another element of purpose, which was giving back - doing something for no other reason than to make the world a better place. I had been coaching minor sports and was actively involved in multiple community organizations. Initially, I thought that was to serve my Community pillar, only to discover this also serves my pillar of Self. Serving others nourishes my soul and helps to restore my mental energy, which, in turn, serves all Three Pillars of a Balanced Life.

I challenge Oxford's definition of purpose in reference to the notion that purpose is static at any point in our lives.

Instead, I encourage you to think of Purpose as something dynamic that changes over time. There will be times when it will be obvious that you are achieving your purpose, making it abundant. At other times you might struggle to see the purpose in your life. This brings me back to my original point about letting purpose find you. In other words, set yourself up by serving your three pillars, doing the things that bring you closer to your dream life, and purpose will find you.

As you encounter adversity on your journey, you will need to draw on your purpose as a means of staying energized, and finding the determination to keep moving forward so like a tank, keep it filled!

Live Intentionally - While going sailing, there was some baggage that I carried. As I have already detailed, I am fascinated by the ocean, but what lurks below scares me. It's dark, vast, and unknown.

The internal conflict caused by this paradox tore at me and gave my Headshaker Self a great deal of ammunition to argue against the idea. It would have been very easy for me to abort the plan and blame any number of things on why we didn't make it happen.

Instead, I decided that I was going to become intentional about living my best life.

I acknowledged that I was accountable to no one other than myself, for better or worse, in making my life's vision a reality.

I started out by developing a plan and a series of executable goals, and I pledged to myself that execution was solely my responsibility.

The idea was that I was in charge of my success. If I needed help, I had a network of people I could go to for support, but, again, it was MY responsibility to keep the plan in motion.

If, at any point, the plan became stalled, it was my responsibility to recognize that and develop strategies to get it back in motion. I wasn't required to execute the entire plan alone but I needed to be solely responsible for keeping it moving and adapting when necessary.

Accountability to Self is the single most impactful behavior we can adopt.

In adopting accountability to Self, we close that loop by taking credit for our own success, and personal responsibility for our shortcomings.

As you ponder this concept, ask yourself if there was a time in your life when you did not achieve the result you desired. Then ask if you held yourself accountable for the result or merely set out to blame the actions of others. Was there an opportunity to hold yourself more accountable, and what might have changed if you did?

Applaud the Experience - Life is not a spectator sport. It's meant to be lived with zest and vigor. Our perspective is a critical influence on the experience we have. When we become intentional about seeing our collective experiences in a positive light, it can change our whole existence.

If you reflect on almost anything significant that you do in life, there are ups and downs. It's natural for us to hold onto the downs, likely because they were the moments that left the biggest scars. When you give yourself permission to let go of the scars and zoom out, chances are you will see that the whole of the experience is much more beautiful than the micro moments of the darkest times.

To pull examples of this in my own life, I can look to my children, and their path to adulthood. I was not a natural at parenting - there were tough moments. Even to this date, I struggle with elements of my relationship with my daughter. However, when I zoom out and look at the whole of the experience, I would not change any of it. It is a part of who I am today, and there are so many beautiful moments, that can easily put the tougher moments into context and enable me to applaud the experience.

Compass Point Reflections:

1) Make A Passion Statement

Detail the things you are passionate about and use that list to create a passion statement. This will assist you to build a life around what is most important to you, rather than trying to salvage things you like from the life you've built.

2) Acknowledge Growth

Acknowledge growth and hold it in a safe place. It is a quantifiable measure of the progress you are making toward your goals. Growth fuels you on your journey towards fulfilment.

3) Shift Your Perspective

In moments of setback or frustration, challenge yourself to shift your perspective from negative to positive.

"If you find yourself in a hole, the first thing to do is stop diggin'." ~ Anonymous

CHAPTER 5 - THE WIND THAT FILLS YOUR SAIL

"Our dilemma is that we hate change and love it at the same time; what we really want is for things to remain the same but get better." - Sydney J. Harris

I came home from Florida, inspired by passions that I had left to flicker out, knowing that my life needed some changes.

I was at a point where I had completely defined myself by my career and the success I had realized. Working almost non-stop while neglecting my family and my own well being, I justified it by identifying it as my purpose. The reality though was that it was a false substitute for purpose. Fortunately, the new VP was the one who taught me this. When he came onboard, he was driven by his own ego. He was determined to convince those around him that he was to be feared no matter how successful they were at their roles in the company. He proved his brilliance by diminishing the ideas and accomplishments of those around him. He taught me that while a corporation can be sympathetic to their employees' well being, it is up to each of us to be the masters of our *own* well being. Ultimately, if we determine our value, and our purpose, by the title on our business card, our job description, or even the results we produce, that is something that can be taken away in a moment. The time for change had come, and now I needed to learn how to change.

Change can be scary and difficult if not managed properly. The first question you must ask yourself is "WHAT?" What will change deliver to your life? The answer to that should serve as your motivation for change. Understanding and embracing it will give you the inspiration needed to carry on when things get tough and the Headshaker starts speaking loudest.

I was at a tipping point in my life. I was maintaining a hectic pace and reaping the rewards of success. But it was like I was running a marathon that had no end. Worse was the fact I was running at a pace I feared I couldn't sustain. The Three Pillars model helped me to realize why change was needed. I perceived that change would allow me to restore balance to my life. That balance would deliver freedom to pursue my passions and embrace a simpler life once again.

I had become obsessed with being Responsible Shawn, the corporate soldier who had refined the art of business development and made it seem purposeful. It was as if I buried myself in work to avoid the question of whether I was living my best life. The vision of sailing communities floating in the Gulf of Mexico just off of Florida's west coast caused me to ask that question. Instantly, I understood why I needed the freedom. This was the simple life I had promised myself. Pursuing this life would enable me to better serve my Self pillar, thereby bringing greater balance to my life.

Until I rediscovered my passion and longing for going sailing and desire to live by the sea, I had not realized how much my Self and Family pillars had been underserved. I had forgotten the time in my life when I directly associated success in my career with a means to pursue passions with my family and larger community. Suddenly, visions of the life I dreamt of were back in focus.

I decided to accept the new venture poised in front of me and become self-employed. I resolved that I could work from anywhere so long as I had a cell phone, laptop, and access to an airport. Why couldn't it be a floating home? A home that could change neighborhoods as the seasons changed. By now, Dreamer Shawn was back at the helm, and my passion was lighting the way.

I left my corporate job, started my own business, and built a team across Canada that became SLH Sales Inc., a national sales agency, representing building materials manufacturers from coast to coast. We began offering building materials to home improvement retailers and distributors.

Responsible Shawn was not entirely happy with the decision but recognized that in my previous corporate role, I was not properly serving my Self or my Family pillars. By acknowledging the importance of each of the three equally balanced pillars, it brought logic to a conversation that made the discussion much easier. Suddenly, I wasn't risking all for a reckless venture. I realized that I had as much, or more to fear, if I didn't pursue this opportunity.

That trip to Florida brought me to discover that the biggest regret I could ever have had nothing to do with money. As I sat alone at night in my hotel room it dawned on me that the biggest regret I could have would be dying alone, full of remorse for not having pursued my passions - the things I enjoy most in life. Or worse, not having a community to share those memories with.

Having brought clarity to my "What" and my "What's next" made this a much easier decision to make. No longer was I paralyzed by thoughts of "what if" because I had identified "what if not" as a greater threat.

After getting a full team on board at SLH Sales, I spent several months getting up to full speed.

I assumed full responsibility for how my business was run including operating costs, and added HR, IT, and accounting to my title. While it was overwhelming at times, the challenge revived me, and with the freedom I gained, I was able to start rebuilding the two other pillars of my life.

Meanwhile, in the background was the decision to go sailing. Determined to not let the passion to die again, I set August 2014 as my deadline.

It's On You

I'll say it again - as you resolve to make changes in your life, know the first step is to appoint yourself as the chief change-maker. This is a critical first step. Acknowledge that change will not happen by chance, it will only happen when you commit to being the one who will drive the change. Throw away excuses and convince yourself that change happens when you draw yourself the map, embrace your compass, and commit to using it, regardless of what adversity you will inevitably face.

Once you have convinced yourself of your ability to affect change, the next step is to start thinking in an action-oriented frame of mind. This means no longer saying "one day" or "I should" and start saying "I will" and "I am".

This is a step I struggled with as I first committed to going sailing. I kept using the terms "IF we go sailing" not "when we go sailing". This told me I wasn't fully committed to the idea. Not long after, I connected with Renee Petrillo, author of *A Sail of Two Idiots* and live aboard sailor. She offered the advice to "just pick a date and commit to it". Once I did that, I found myself speaking in the "I am". Suddenly, the process got much smoother. I was no longer wasting energy trying to convince myself. This allowed me to make plans without having a back door to them - a means of escape if I suddenly convinced myself it was a terrible idea. Picking a date was the first step to becoming fully committed, even if it got me fully committed!

The Enemy Within

An enemy you will surely face, and who will likely give you the greatest battle, comes from within. The Headshaker Self in all of us despises change and lives in negativity. Most of us have become conditioned to believe in the 9-5 to 65 mentality and its ability to keep us "safe". When you venture outside of that notion, the Responsible Self becomes speechless, which lends opportunity to the Headshaker to become loud and obnoxious.

The best way to counter this is to get the Dreamer Self and Responsible Self to collaborate. This is accomplished by using compromise, and the "Inventory of Facts Method" whenever you encounter worry or doubt. This method requires that you calmly analyze any fear that haunts you by asking, "What do I know to be a fact?".

For example, as we planned our sailing journey, I worried about whether we could lose everything if we sank our boat. By focussing on facts, I reminded myself of the following:

   1) Our boat would be covered by insurance.

2) We would not venture off the dock if the weather predictions advised against it.

3) When we did venture off the dock, I would always plan safe ports that we could duck into if necessary.

Your mind works on two types of data: fact, and thought. It's easy for us to become absorbed, or even obsessed by thought, if we don't discipline ourselves. As you process your thoughts ask yourself if it is fact or unsubstantiated thinking. In doing so you can silence much of the things that cause unnecessary fear and gain the clarity to properly deal with the possibilities that deserve attention. When you come to those possibilities, be prepared to use compromise. If there is a possibility that is fact based, which there is little opportunity to avoid, use compromise to find a way to meet the objective, while satisfying both your Responsible Self and Dreamer Self.

In my example, I feared what we would do if we had a mechanical breakdown while at sea. Using a logical, factual approach to consider this possibility, I rationalized options that I would employ:

1) I could sail to a safe port.
2) I could radio for help.

3) If my sail was also disabled, the vessel typically was not in danger except for when it was close to shore, a reef, or other shallow waters, in which case I could drop anchor. The forces driving me to those shallow waters would cause my anchor to snag firm before damage could occur.

Option 3 was not ideal to either my Dreamer Self, nor my Responsible Self, but was one compromise that would make peace between two differing points of view.

There is no possible way to have a plan for all things that could disrupt your progress, but having contingencies for some of the most likely scenarios helps you to quiet most thought storms and rationalize the Dreamer and Responsible Self points of view.

For Whom the Change Tolls

In 1940 Ernest Hemingway wrote the book *For Whom The Bell Tolls*. Without doing a deep dive into the plot, the Bell is said to represent death of an individual, relevant to how it affects us all in the greater community.

To that point I propose that Change represents rebirth. So it stands to reason that when you choose to make a change in your life is to ask yourself, "for whom are you making the change?". As we've discussed, change can be scary, challenging, and disruptive. We resist change for these reasons, and many more. The ONLY person we should ever make change for is ourselves. While change, or rebirth will have an impact on your greater community, focus on the change you require. You can consider possible effects at a later point.

When I met Leanne, she inspired me to become a better man. She helped me to see that I was stuck, and as a result of being stuck, I had some bad habits. I had a short temper, was judgemental, obsessed with my career, and had neglected the well-being of my Self, and Family/Community pillars.

The important element here is that she inspired me to see these things in myself. She has never asked me to change. She has loved me for who I am.

While Leanne inspired me to be a better man, I was the one who recognized that my life would improve if I started using the principles of the Three Pillars model to restore balance to my life.

As I committed attention to my Self pillar, and to healing myself, my temperamental outbursts happened less often, and I learned to manage them much better. As I learned to react with curiosity rather than judgement, I was able to look at differences of opinion from the other person's perspective, making it much easier to resolve disagreements. Naturally, this choice to change improved things in all three pillars of my life, particularly the quality of relationships that were most important to me. This was a decision that I made, for myself, and embraced because of that.

There have been times, when the process of change has been difficult, that I have been tempted to blame others for the challenges I've faced. By recognizing that I was making change for myself, it made it possible for me to recognize that the challenges of change, were challenges that I signed up for of my own volition.

As you commit to your own change, be sure that you commit to change ONLY for yourself. As it becomes difficult, look at yourself in the mirror, and own responsibility for the challenge, and remind yourself of the rewards that await you on the other side.

Compass Point Reflections:

1) Know Your What

Change can be challenging, it can be scary, and it can be demanding of your energy and attention. At some point, you will ask yourself "is it worth it?".

Take the time to define the "what" in your life will improve if you commit to making the change. This will answer that question for you. Use that statement as motivation through every step of your journey.

2) Be the reason for and the driver of change

When you commit to making change to your life, do it for yourself - no one else. It's okay to get your inspiration to change from others, but to be fully committed, you must be the one you are making the change for. Likewise, you must be the one who is in the driver's seat of change. Anything less will be setting yourself up to fail.

3) Adopt a change perspective

"One day" can be one of the greatest enemies of change. It serves us almost as permission to put off change indefinitely. Shift "one day" or "I should" to "I will" then "I am" and move beyond.

"The first step toward change is awareness. The second step is acceptance." ~ Nathaniel Branden

CHAPTER 6 - DREAMLESS SEAS

"You know you're in love when you can't fall asleep because reality is finally better than your dreams." ~ Dr. Seuss

As long as I can remember, I've always been a dreamer. Although I went through a phase of my life where Responsible Shawn took over and called the shots almost exclusively, Dreamer Shawn was never dead. He simply became a loner in the corner so to speak. What I forgot was that you only get one shot to live a life, and there are a great number of ways to make it meaningful, purposeful, and fulfilling. Being responsible gets you in the game, but seldom is it, on its own, enough to build a life fully lived!

After I committed to making change, I re-defined my dream, and committed to pursuing it. It was the spring of 2014 by that point. My son was scheduled to finish high school that June and had no idea what was next for him. He struggled in school, so the one thing he was sure of was a lack of desire to spend three or four more years in a classroom setting. So, I pitched to Leanne that the three of us would go sailing and bring our two Alaskan Malamutes. In my view, Daeyten would get life lessons that would prove more valuable than anything taught in a classroom.

To say Leanne was an easy sell would be an understatement. While she wasn't a longtime sailor, the appeal of life on the seas, and a winter in sandals was an adventure she had no desire to miss.

My son was a tougher sell. I reflected on myself at that age and could only recall the Dreamer Shawn who dreamt of selling t-shirts on the beach. I had forgotten how quickly Dreamer Shawn became silent and Responsible Shawn took over.

Although Daeyten was barely 18, it seemed that his Responsible Self was already dominant. He was convinced that he needed to build a career before his last day of high school. He had no idea what that career looked like or how he was going to figure it out. He just knew that he would. I proposed that going sailing would give him some time to figure that out - no pressure. Long story short, by July, he became fully committed to going sailing.

The previous summer, we had purchased a 33' Hunter sailboat and had learned just enough to be only a little dangerous. So what was left to do was to discover how to make the transition from weekend cruisers to full time live aboards.

From the moment we committed to going sailing, life became more enjoyable. I saw that I was working toward goals that served me at higher levels. We all need food and shelter to survive, but if we don't serve ourselves, we struggle to thrive. In making the decision to go sailing, and having my wife as a partner, all the work I was doing in my career and elsewhere made sense and gave purpose. Success in your career is a form of purpose, but on its own, it becomes one-dimensional. For most, there comes a day when your career is no longer a part of your daily life, so more than ever, you need the other pillars to hold you up.

In April 2014 we listed our investment property for sale to help finance the transition to our new life. In July, when the investment property remained unsold, we decided to list our home for sale as well. When my son announced that he wanted to bring friend Jonny along for the adventure, suddenly our two cabin 33' sailboat seemed a bit small. So, we listed it for sale as well, hoping we could upgrade to a larger vessel.

With less than three months till departure day, we had three "homes" listed for sale, and none were selling. This was a classic moment where my Headshaker self was having a fantastic time ridiculing me - until suddenly all were sold. I used the inventory of facts method faithfully to tune out the Headshaker until then.

As you commit to making a change in your life, it's important for you to imagine what an ideal life looks like and embrace that vision. Envision it through your eyes only, being sure to pay attention to the details. I can't emphasize it enough that this vision should be through YOUR eyes. Do not allow the biases of an unimaginative society to limit your dream life. I dare you to dream like there are no limits. The challenge here is to dream about the things that will give your life meaning, purpose, and fulfillment. Do not let your dreams become hijacked by shiny things that won't bring you true fulfillment. For many, our first instinct is to imagine a life with a bigger house, nicer car, a cottage, or vacation home in the Caribbean, merely because that's what everyone says they would buy if they won the lottery. Now is the time to give serious focus to what really matters to you. What life will snap you out of stuck and leave you waking up each morning happy, fulfilled, and looking forward to the day - a day of meaning and purpose?

Don't expect this process to be simple or come naturally. Determining exactly what an ideal life should look like is one of the hardest parts of change. It's also one of the biggest reasons why so many people fail to live their dream life. They know their life is far from perfect, but they simply can't bring into focus what a perfect life would be like for them.

One reason why this happens is the "Not Worthy" effect. Simply put, most people don't consider themselves to be worthy of a life full of their wildest aspirations. To most, it would be as extreme as going to a restaurant and ordering one of everything!

Instead, we rationalize that we could never become the CEO of a company, or could never become a professional athlete, or could never travel to every country in the world. We tell ourselves "that's simply not practical from the place that we are". forgetting that to achieve any feat of greatness, it always starts with a first step and simply requires more steps. We all come from the same place and end up in the same place. The brilliance of the picture we paint, between those two points, depends entirely on our ability to dream and embrace those dreams.

Beware of Limiting Beliefs

For much of my adult life, I never imagined that I could live on a boat and travel south once the butter got cold and stopped melting. That is, never - until I saw people doing it and realized that they were no different than me.

You could say the same about so many limitations we put on ourselves in life. While there are gifted athletes who seem destined to be superstars from the moment they lace up skates or pick up a football, most athletes get to the pro level because of three things:

1) They dared to dream a dream;
2) They chose to believe in that dream, and;
3) They put the work in!

For you to dream, you first need to become aware of what limits your dreams and then remove those limits from your mentality.

For me, it was my conditioning to become responsible that was limiting me. I grew up telling anyone who would listen that I was going to live a simple life, selling t-shirts on the beach, learning to surf, and be at one with the ocean. But as soon as I discovered I was going to be a dad, my Responsible Self took over, and my dream of a simpler life evaporated. There was no compromise - my conditioning took over, and I completely abandoned the life I originally envisioned.

My first mistake was that I failed to believe in my dream. My second mistake was inflexibility. I convinced myself that there was only one way to be a father, and that was to do it the same way my father did - as Mr. Responsible. The problem was I wasn't my father. I was nowhere near as good at being responsible as he was.

I absolutely don't regret having lived the life I did before I discovered the three pillars model. But I'm more grateful that I discovered my need for balance when I did.

The Fear Factor

Once you discover what is limiting you, you need to think about what feeds those limits and how to overcome them.

Fear is the single most significant reason why people never dare to pursue their dreams. The saddest part is that many don't even realize this to be the case. They convince themselves that life is good, and that nothing needs to change, because somewhere in a deep recess of their psyche, the belief exists that change is scary and could go horribly wrong. Admitting to the possibility of a better life, and choosing to pursue it, means having to come face to face with the horrible beast called change.

I believe my biggest fear - the one that allowed me to live wholly in the Responsible Shawn persona for so long - was the fear of being a bad dad. I became a father much sooner than planned, and I had little time to consider what being a dad required - or meant. I convinced myself that if I was anything less than a completely responsible adult, I would be a horrible dad. I imagined not being able to provide for my family and resolved that that was the worst thing that could ever happen. Ironically, I got so busy trying to be a responsible adult, I undermined my desire to be a good dad, in underserving my Self and family pillars.

Overcoming your fears, and limiting beliefs, is not a quick and easy process. You must start by clearly understanding what drives these emotions.

In attempting to better understand what influences human behavior Swiss psychiatrist Carl Jung developed what is known as the Jungian shadow. Drawn from the Very Well Mind website, comes this explanation:

> *"The shadow exists as part of the unconscious mind and is composed of repressed ideas, weaknesses, desires, instincts, and shortcomings.*
>
> *The shadow forms out of our attempts to adapt to cultural norms and expectations. It is this archetype that contains all of the things that are unacceptable not only to society, but also to one's own personal morals and values. It might include things such as envy, greed, prejudice, hate, and aggression."*

Put in simpler terms, Dr. Jung believed that our conscious minds naturally try to block ideas that are not generally accepted by society meaning they exist only in the shadow.

What this means is that if you work to overpower this you are likely to meet more resistance from within. Instead, you must come to understand your fears, and your conditioned beliefs that you keep hidden from your consciousness. You might benefit by talking to someone who can help you explore your thoughts and emotions, such as a psychologist, to help you understand them better.

Once you understand your fears, and the limiting beliefs that hold you back, remove judgement, and become curious about why they exist. That understanding will help to navigate past them. You might also use the Inventory of Facts Method that we discussed in Chapter Four.

Make a point of acknowledging the fears you have. Rather than shoving them into the recesses of your mind, process the validity of them, as well as the level of threat the factual ones present. Then consider how that threat can be avoided. For a threat that can't be avoided, consider the best and worst-case scenario.

As morbid as it may sound, as I contemplated selling my home and going sailing, I imagined that the worst-case scenario would be drowning at sea. Given my fear of deep water, this possibility terrified me. While it was a possibility, after I considered how likely or unlikely that was, I then compared it to the alternative - not going sailing. When I considered the idea of not going sailing, and instead choosing a safer life, it seemed much more threatening to me. I envisioned the alternative as slowly drowning in a mediocre existence - a betrayal of the life I once envisioned. I determined I would rather risk an early death from living than a slow death from merely existing. Once I had come to terms with what I saw as the worst-case scenario, confronting my lesser fears suddenly seemed more manageable.

Let Fear Work for You

A huge motivating force that got me started down the path of change, ironically, was fear. Multiple people my age had met with unfortunate, early ends to their lives. A buddy that I went to school with became a victim of depression, and another died of cancer.

I woke up one morning faced with the reality that my tomorrows were not guaranteed, and fear hit me. *What will it feel like if I suddenly find myself lying on my death bed, with so many items on my bucket list still unchecked?* I pondered.

Then I asked myself:

"How will my children rationalize my life and use it to inspire theirs if my greatest legacy was living a safe life?"

It was then that I dreamed the most significant dream I could dream. I dreamed that I would, from that day forward, live a life that would leave lasting memories. In this dream, I pledged that no matter when my final breath came, my mind would be fuller of great memories than it would be of regrets. All I had to figure out next was how to do that! Which brings us back to Dare to Dream.

Daring To Dream 101

So now I pass that challenge to you. How will you dream a dream that will give you a life of purpose and meaning, leading to fulfillment?

1) Think

Do some thinking. This sounds cliché, but it's actually not at all. I want you to set time aside each day to just think. I don't want you to think about anything in particular - just think.

What's important will come to you. All you need to do is have an open mind.

If you find yourself thinking about tasks you need to complete or bills that need to be paid, silence those thoughts. Open your mind to thoughts about what you enjoy most in life. Think about great times in your past and consider what made those memories so great. Think about past activities you enjoyed that aren't a part of your life now, that you miss. Think about activities in your life you particularly enjoy and wish you could do more.

Responsible Self will try to intervene by telling you things like "there are only so many hours in a day" and that "you can't do activity ABC all at the time". Silence that voice. This moment isn't the time for practicality. This time is to be held exclusively for Dreamer Self. No limits, no boundaries, no conditions. I want you to be truly imaginative. This is what is often referred to as "blue-sky thinking".

Naturally, you'll find yourself wondering how to find the time to commit to blue-sky thinking every day.

The answer is simple… "Pay yourself first". This is a critical element of the principles of the Three Pillars of a Balanced Life. The most important pillar is your Self pillar, and it is the foundation that supports the whole concept of a balanced life.

So, committing an hour per day is critical to the well-being of all three pillars. If you commute to work, this is as simple as turning off the radio and leaving yourself to your thoughts. Be sure to bring a notepad and capture your ideas on paper once you've arrived at your destination. Do so before you enter the office to ensure the frame of mind doesn't escape you as you are greeted by your co-workers.

If you are a remote worker, you can simply make a point of starting your day an hour earlier, turning off your phone, and closing your office door. Or perhaps you can use your lunch hour to be alone with your thoughts, while taking a walk.

The most important point here is to commit the time to doing nothing but thinking about positive possibilities for one hour each day.

2) Mirror Others

Observing others who inspire you is another great way to envision your dream life. Perhaps this is someone you've met, someone you know of, or it's a public personality whom you admire.

Think about what it is about their life that causes you to admire them, or their life. Think about what is transferable to you. What can you learn from them, and what elements of their life do you already have?

Do research on them to better understand their story and how they got the life that you admire. Then, think about the things you would change if you were going to re-create their life.

The key I want you to remember is to ask yourself, "What would change in your life if your life had those components you admire in others?". Always be sure to consider if and how those components will bring deeper meaning to your life. Which pillar or pillars will they serve? The reason you need to do this is because the answer is what will motivate you to seek change.

By contrast, an easy way to whittle down what your dream life should look like is to also reflect on people whose lives you don't believe are for you.

For me, Joe in Accounting was a life I found easy to eliminate. I knew very early on that accounting was never going to be for me. I'm a big picture guy, who needs to be creative and experience variety.

It's important when developing your dream career or dream life that you give firm consideration to where small steps will likely take you.

If you take the time to talk to people, many will proclaim to you, "This isn't the way it was supposed to be". I know, I'm married to one. In chapter 4 I told you about my wife Leanne and her 29 year 'temporary job' at the YMCA. While she has many great memories, and lasting friendships, the *"what if"* lingers.

When you come across people who live lives that you find unappealing, it is just as important to note the negative characteristics as it is to note things you admire about one's life.

When I entered the business world, I was a sponge. I would observe all types of people around me. When I got into sales, I had the opportunity to work with many sales managers, and I kept a catalogue of what I considered the strengths and weaknesses of each. Then I tried to learn and emulate the strengths that I admired most. I would go to shows where I got the opportunity to chat with other vendor sales reps and discover what their roles were like. I would find out what their products were, what their sales territories were, and what their bosses were like.

I used all of this to define my ideal career role. The unfortunate part was that I didn't put the same amount of energy into understanding if/how they achieved a balanced life until much later.

3) Ask Your Younger Self!

By the time I became a father, at twenty-five years old, I had committed the cardinal sin of thinking younger

Shawn wasn't qualified to weigh in on the path I was going to take with my life.

If you think of our various stages of life as different people, with young Shawn (5-10) being one person, and early teen Shawn (10-15) and adolescent Shawn (15-20) and so on…three of the four Shawns to that point had similar idea of how I was going to live life - chasing dreams, selling t-shirts on the beach, seeing the world. I completely ignored that advice.

Perhaps it was mid-life crisis Shawn that shook things up, but it was a good shake-up!

Don't make the same mistake.

Our younger selves lack maturity, but we have innocence, and we are much freer of limiting beliefs. Our younger selves are adventurous, imaginative, and bold enough to still think we can change the world. Listen to that voice as you dare to dream!

With that, go and be free. Free to think and free to dream. Go to a quiet place where you won't be interrupted and listen to yourself. Create a vision of what your best life looks like, so we can continue the process together of you achieving that life!

Power Of Perseverance

There's a saying: "It's always darkest just before dawn". What that meant to me was the value of perseverance and belief in yourself in whatever mission you set out to accomplish.

In July 2014, we had a home, an investment property, and our boat for sale. We were getting very frustrated that nothing was selling and were prepared to abandon the plan. We actually set a deadline and were one week away when our home, our investment property, and our boat all sold. To this day I reflect on how our life might be if we had allowed our doubts to choose the course of action and cancel our plans.

At that moment, we had little time to reflect. We were suddenly faced with no where to live come September 30! We immediately developed a plan to find a bigger boat. It was early August by now, so we essentially had to find something in the Annapolis area or south, since there was not time to sail anything from Canada before the weather turned cold.

We put offers in on two boats, but neither worked out. As the calendar turned to September, we were barely four weeks away and still boatless. While we weren't desperate, we were quickly becoming familiar with the concept! Feeling our options were more limited by the day, we decided to rent a motorhome, pack all of our boating supplies into it, and drive it to Annapolis, Maryland, where we would live until we found the right boat. Annapolis was home to the largest boat show in the northeast US and widely regarded as a major boating hub. We believed it was our best shot at finding the right boat.

One week before leaving for Annapolis, we had most of our things either staged to be packed in the RV or already packed in a storage container. That's when we got news that Jonny, Daeyten's buddy, was no longer joining us. One can speculate on many reasons why, but my best guess is it just didn't feel right for him. Life would have been simpler if he had made that decision before we sold our first boat, but we sensed it was all working out as it was meant to be.

On September 30, we were packed. We managed to crunch our entire lives into a 10x10 storage container and 30' motorhome. We even managed to fit the three of us, the two dogs, along with Leanne's parents and my parents. Imagine seven people and two large dogs co-existing in the RV until we found a boat. We brought the parents because we needed someone to drive the RV back once we found a boat. The one-way charge was out of the question!

When we decided to invite the parents, for that reason, we struggled to determine which ones to ask. There was one right answer, so I proposed we ask both. *"I'm certain they won't all want to come"* I reasoned. Turns out that having a child buy a boat and sailing away is a major event in many parents' lives. Either they wanted to witness firsthand if we were really that crazy, or they wanted to make sure we found one that floated. They all came.

As we crossed the border into the US, in the RV I spoke to the border services agent. He was a very matter of fact gentleman who seemed to be very bored in his work that day. He asked the routine questions, showing little emotion, until he asked "where are you going" and "what for".

When I responded that we were going to Annapolis, and we were going to buy a boat, and go sailing, I had to be sure to answer in convincing fashion. Until that moment I knew full well that that was the plan, but it was as if I still had a secret back door plan. If we didn't find the right boat, we could always go back. At that moment, the agent's demeanor completely changed. He suddenly lit up. His expression went from droll to excited. It was as if I just woke his dream self from a long slumber. He asked about my sailing experience, and if I had served in the Navy. Seeing him come alive and buy into our plan helped me to realize that we were doing this, and we weren't crazy! The plan might have been less than perfect, but we were doing it!

Perhaps what was most significant to me in that moment was my father had accompanied us. I knew since the first moment I had mentioned to him our plan to leave the corporate world and go sailing, a part of him wanted to shake me sane. But I also saw a glimmer in his eye that clearly showed he got it. While he may never have fully understood what compelled me to take such an unorthodox path, I got the sense he wished he could. His agreeing to spend an indefinite amount of time with us in a small, rented motorhome clearly showed he was trying. It meant the world to me! It proved to me that supporters will be there for you even when you least expect it! Don't judge or be skeptical. Embrace it!

Compass Point Reflections:

1) Identify Your Limiting Beliefs

Ask yourself what has been holding you back and develop a plan to break through those barriers.

2) Commit To Daily Blue-Sky Thinking

Commit to thinking without limitations as you develop dreams of the greatest possibilities. Put practicality aside for now.

3) Include All Generations of Self In Forming Your Vision

Consider all possibilities, including dreams you had in every phase of your life. Let your inner child shine!

"Twenty years from now, you will be more disappointed by the things that you didn't do than by the ones you did do. So, throw off the bowlines. Sail away from the safe harbor. Catch the trade winds in your sails. Explore. Dream. Discover."

~ H. Jackson Brown Jr., Author of *P.S. I Love You*

CHAPTER 7 - UNTANGLE YOUR ANCHOR

"If you want something you have never had, you must be willing to do something you have never done."

~ Thomas Jefferson

As I pondered the adventure that awaited us I reflected back to when I went out to Banff Alberta, just after college. It wasn't lost on me that that adventure was also about pursuing a simpler life. It would have been easy to conclude that my 'wrong turn' in life happened when I returned from Alberta, sold my VW van and abandoned my dream of a laid-back hippy lifestyle. I could have even blamed my dad for the traditional family values he impressed on me.

Instead, I owned up to the choices that I made and admitted that my life didn't suck. It simply needed some changes - changes that were within my capabilities. I needed growth, and I knew that the moment had arrived, to start making the changes happen.

When we arrived in Annapolis we had showings set up for two catamarans, either of which we hoped would be suitable for our future home. Both turned out to be much less than expected. These boats were the short list. Any other catamaran that was on the market in the Annapolis area had already been eliminated for not satisfying our checklist. With seven people, and two dogs living in such a small space, I knew our window of time was very finite. A change of plan was needed. I asked the boat broker to expand his list of options to all boats in the area that were 15 years or newer, and 37' or longer, with three cabins. The criteria no longer excluded monohulls. We met back that afternoon, and he presented about a dozen options. After quickly whitling the list down, we settled on two to look at: a 2004 Beneteau 393 and a 2002 Beneteau 421. Both were boats that came out of charter, listed at $89,000. The 421 had clear signs of the wear and tear of a charter boat, while the 393 was incredibly clean for a charter boat. Even more appealing to us was the new replacement engine with only 400 hours on her. We struck a deal and worked at hyper speed to get the survey done and put a new bottom on her.

Get Off the Rumble Strip

Until we struck the deal for the Beneteau 393 and finalized it doubt continued to creep in about whether we could make it happen. Before making the decision to go on this adventure it seemed that my life had become just comfortable enough that I didn't want to risk screwing it up - radical change was a no-go zone! To that point in my life, I had become accustomed to living on the rumble strip. You know that grooved spot on the side of some highways that's designed to make driving uncomfortable so that if you begin to drift off, it alerts you? Metaphorically that seemed to be my life.

It happens to all of us at some point, where we come to accept that living on the rumble strip is what life is meant to be. I accepted that whenever I experienced gains, loss always seemed to be close behind. If I got an unexpected bonus, the car would break down. I was existing, but not thriving. While I was getting ahead, it seemed to be two steps forward and one back. Momentum seemed to elude me. It was almost as if I feared that if I dared to expect more, somehow, the universe would punish me and take it all away.

As someone who takes tremendous pride in being able to control my own destiny, this concept of life on the rumble strip was a contrast that was rather difficult to rationalize. It was like a mystical force I dared not challenge for fear of making things worse. Then I read about Learned Helplessness.

Learned Helplessness

As I researched this phenomenon I came across information about a condition called "Learned Helplessness" (LH).

First, I must point out that I am not a certified psychologist, and as such, I don't want to get too deep into this, but let me explain Learned Helplessness as best I can in layman's terms.

Learned Helplessness is a phenomenon that was discovered in the late 1960's through experiments conducted by psychologists Martin Seligman and Steven Maier.

Learned helplessness is observed in both humans and other animals when they have been conditioned to expect pain, suffering, or discomfort without a way to escape it, whereby after enough conditioning, they will stop trying to avoid the pain altogether - even if there is an opportunity to truly escape it.

Learned helplessness often occurs in response to stressful situations or traumatic experiences in which a person feels they have limited control over the outcome.

This leads to feelings of helplessness and a loss of motivation, which remain even once they have the opportunity to make changes to their circumstances. Sadly, studies show that it is rather common that learned helplessness can spiral a person into a state of depression.

While I will present to you some ways to combat learned helplessness, I must first say that if you believe that you may have already spiraled into a state of depression, I encourage you to seek the assistance of a qualified mental health professional to help you cope and recover. Like any mental health condition, depression is not a sign of weakness. It is simply an illness that approximately 15-30% of the population experiences at some point in their life. It's treatable, but early treatment is the best course of action!

Some symptoms of depression are:

- Feeling sad or having a depressed mood;
- Loss of interest or pleasure in activities once enjoyed;

- Changes in appetite – weight loss or gain unrelated to dieting;
- Trouble sleeping or sleeping too much;
- Loss of energy or increased fatigue;
- Increase in purposeless physical activity (e.g., inability to sit still, pacing, handwringing) or slowed movements or speech (these actions must be severe enough to be observable by others);
- Feeling worthless or guilty;
- Difficulty thinking, concentrating, or making decisions;
- Thoughts of death or suicide.

If you are affected by learned helplessness, you will likely find yourself checking off some or all of the following boxes:

- Feeling a lack of control over the outcome of situations;
- Failing to ask for help;
- Having low self-esteem;
- Decreased motivation;
- Putting less effort into tasks;
- Lack of persistence;
- Feelings of frustration;

- Passivity;
- Giving up easily.

This explained the hopelessness I had been feeling had a name, which drove me to seek change in my life. Knowing that others had gotten stuck, just as I did, helped me to realize it was within my control to do something about it. The fact others had freed themselves provided me the motivation to resume control of my life.

If you recognize some or all of these symptoms, this is your wake-up call! If I could escape, so can you! If you're not sure if this is your struggle, call on the most trusted members of your family/community and ask for their feedback. Do they notice some of these symptoms in you? The closest members of your network are as or more likely than you to notice patterns in your behavior.

If you do feel you are stuck here, the first option is, of course a professional - a psychologist, certified counselor, or life/executive coach. If you don't feel that is necessary, here are some strategies you can deploy on your own:

1) Control The Likelihood of the Outcome
As you embark on your mission, start with simpler tasks that are most likely to elicit a favorable outcome.

This will build the confidence within you to take on the more challenging tasks, with the confidence that you control the outcome. As you achieve small successes you will develop the sense that you control your own destiny. Doing so builds momentum toward larger successes.

2) Temper Your Desire For Preferred Outcomes

While we all desire the ideal outcome, refrain from believing that success in a given action is of absolute necessity or the only possible path to overall success. Prepare yourself for the notion that you might not achieve your ideal outcome every time and learn that that is acceptable. Ultimately the only thing in life that we can't ever recover from is death. Know that any adverse outcome, short of death, always presents you with the opportunity to learn, re-group and refine your methods.

3) Focus On That Which You Can Control

There will always be circumstances that reside beyond your control. Some might be permanently beyond your control, while others may be temporary. Focus on the things you can control and be wise enough to know the difference.

4) Celebrate the Good and Quarantine the Rest

When you don't achieve the desired result, be realistic about the cause, and then quarantine it. If the negative result happened because of external circumstances beyond your control, acknowledge that rather than beating yourself up. Isolate the specific problems within your control that were the cause of the negative result and focus on improving those. Do not allow one negative event to be exaggerated into a sense of global failure.

At the same time, when successful outcomes are as the result of inherent strengths, embrace and celebrate what helped you realize that desired outcome. Acknowledge the specific skill sets that you brought to the process, which contributed to your success.

Clear Your Head of Clutter

As we prepared to leave Annapolis, and begin sailing south, I resolved to leave the *rumble strip* (Learned Helplessness) thinking at the dock. As the captain of a vessel with four other living creatures aboard, I needed to assert a strong sense of control of my destiny. Gone, but not forgotten - I deliberately pledged to not entirely eliminate the *rumble strip beast*. I knew that I needed to take my life off autopilot and hold myself to account for our success. The rumble strip beast represented a complacency that drove me to mediocrity. Completely erasing all memory of that complacency would leave little to keep me from drifting back there in the future. It's often said "those who don't know history are doomed to repeat it".

I wanted to remain conscious of the possibility of encountering things beyond my control but learn the difference between those and things I can control. All while being deliberate about not drifting back onto the rumble strip. As I experienced doubts, I would again use the Inventory of Fact method to navigate them.

The day was October 10, 2014. We had prepped the boat, had a nice dinner the night previous, with our parents. Now it was time to bid them farewell. It was Canadian Thanksgiving weekend, and they had pledged to be home for celebrations with other family. Likely, they had also had enough of seven people and two dogs living in that rented RV! More importantly, we had run out of excuses to not move on in our journey.

As we bid them farewell, I got my first direct glance at how intimidating this next step was. While I had worked hard to overcome my limiting beliefs, fear of the unknown still stood in front of me. I felt like the ball player, standing at the plate in game 7 of the playoffs. I had left the dock many times before. I knew what to do, and how to do it, but this was different. Suddenly it seemed like it was for all the marbles.

We left the dock the next day at 7am - or tried to. Turns out Daeyten had his own ideas on how to launch. We had never been moored to a dock where we were tied to pilings before. We had also never launched in a situation where wind was opposing current. All that to say, our inexperience showed in glowing fashion. As we struggled to get free, the boat started to drift sideways in the slip, and our voices began to rise.

As captain I had a plan, and as "self-appointed captain" my son had a different plan. I refused to compromise, as did he. The end result was that no one died, and our departure was postponed by a day. I'm sure it also made for interesting chatter among the real sailors that heard us, across the entire Annapolis area.

When a weather system rolled in, we were delayed by another two days. The lesson we learned was that while there are many ways to complete a task, success only comes when those completing the task set aside ego and the need to be right, find compromise, and a willingness to work together. Three days later we left at first light working together in unison and waking no one from bickering.

The most remarkable part of our unexpected delay came in the afternoon of the first day. We were below deck, making lunch, when someone knocked on our boat. It was our boat neighbor who had the same model boat as us. They had just purchased a new canvass bimini and dodger for their boat.

They heard we were headed south and noticed we had no dodger. The purpose of the dodger is to deflect the wind from the cockpit when you're at the helm. It serves an important purpose.

Our boat neighbor offered us their old dodger, including fittings, at no charge. While we wanted to purchase a dodger, it would have needed to be custom made. We did not have time to wait for that. This blessing from someone who was a complete stranger to us came as a remarkable surprise. It was as if the universe had a plan to teach us a lesson about working together while rewarding us for our ability to learn - or it was just a wonderful coincidence!

When we finally did get off the dock, the fear that I feared never really materialized. As we worked together, we eased out of our slip, through the mooring field, and were out into Chesapeake Bay uneventfully.

For a seasoned sailor, none of this would have been a remarkable accomplishment. But we were far from meeting the seasoned sailor bar. I had lots of sailing experience in my small Sea Snark, along with a few years pulling lines as crew on race boats. But we had only one year experience captaining our own motorized vessel, all in calmer waters. This boat was new to us, and we were now dealing with currents and tides. It was a new world for us. But we discovered that the fear of fear was greater than the things we had to fear. It seems that there's no greater way to discover that than to step off whatever cliff it is that you fear stepping off of and spread your wings.

As we got out onto Chesapeake Bay and set a southerly course for Norfolk, we were met with an overwhelming sense of "we've got this!". There was still much to do, and real risks in play but we were no longer restlessly being haunted by fear. Instead, we were using what knowledge we had in order to confront real time situations as they occurred. In essence, we were too busy living in reality to give thought to fear of possibility!

Compass Point Reflections:

1) Get Off the Rumble Strip

As you work to clear your mind, self-doubt will almost certainly creep into your thoughts. It is critical to take a facts-based approach to assessing any threat to your plan. The human mind makes regular practice of creeping thoughts into your consciousness, disguising them as reality. Make a point of always asking yourself if it is fact or thought-based.

2) The First Step

The first step is always the toughest to take, but it's also the most important. Once you take it, the momentum begins. For inspiration, I encourage you to look up *Admiral McRaven and his book, Make Your Bed*

"Life begins at the end of your comfort zone." ~ Neale Donald Walsch

CHAPTER 8 - SELLING YOUR VISION

"Vision is the art of seeing what is invisible to others." ~ Jonathan Swift

When I developed the exciting dream to start my own business, then sell everything, and go sailing, what was obvious was that I had to sell my wife on this vision. I had been away for six days in Florida, in February. All the while she endured a 3-day snowstorm, having had to shovel out 20" of snow. I envisioned coming home smiley and giggly blurting out, "Honey, I have a plan! We're selling everything and going sailing!".

I sensed that my face would feel her response first - either as a kiss or more likely a firm back hand!

Truth be told, she was a relatively easy sell. What I failed to realize was that even though the concept was my idea, I was a tougher sell. On the surface, the romantic vision of living on a boat seemed wonderfully simple. But it took a lot of effort to silence the Headshaker and find compromise between Responsible Shawn and Dreamer Shawn.

We all have partners who we must deal with. In the corporate world, it can be your boss, your customer, the president, the shareholders, or countless other possible stakeholders.

In this case, it was my wife, my Headshaker, and my Responsible Self. I had a disruptive idea that I was emotionally attached to. My Dreamer Self could easily see the advantages of the idea and felt it needed no selling. That's because Dreamer Self was controlling my thoughts and was emotionally attached.

In the previous chapter, I discussed how I overcame what held me back, so let's move on to Leanne. While I knew she had had enough of winter, I recognized that she didn't get to see firsthand the beauty and romance of people living their lives in perpetual warmth. She wasn't emotionally attached yet. Though I knew she was romanced by all of these things, asking her to radically change her life for them was unknown territory. I could not expect her to automatically make the connection that I made even though her first reaction was "sure!". What I needed to do was provide her the clarity that would enable her to see my vision just as I did.

Many in this situation feel that flattery will, as the saying goes, get you everywhere. I could have brought home roses, made her a nice dinner, and raved about how beautiful she must have looked all the while that she was shoveling the 20" of snow. That too would have likely landed me in the ER. As Dale Carnegie once wrote, "Flattery is telling other people exactly what he thinks of himself.". It is often seen as a transparent and manipulative attempt to win one's favor. It typically only serves to raise one's suspicions about your motives.

Instead, I waited until the Friday I returned, and I brought home flowers. I presented them to her apologetically. Then I acknowledged the hard work she put in, getting the driveway cleared while also attending to the other rigors of the week. This simple sign of appreciation eased her tension which was brought on by being trapped in a winter wonderland while I was down south, enjoying the sun. The fact it was from a boardroom window was of no consequence to her.

I told her we were going to a nice restaurant and offered to buy her whatever she wanted that was on the menu. In spite of having just won my third consecutive Chairman's Club Award of Sales Excellence, and a nice bonus to go with it, her Dutch side kept her from taking advantage of my benevolence.

As we dined, I asked her if she knew what purpose was, and whether she felt she had purpose in her life?

As expected, she admitted that her 29 years at the YMCA blessed her with many things - she didn't count an abundance of purpose among them.

Building Bridges

In order to win over a potential partner, you must first come to the process with a curiosity about your partner's wants, needs, and the way they think. Before speaking your first words, you must have done your research to have as good an understanding as possible of what motivates this person as well as what challenges he/she faces. As the conversation progresses, you must be prepared to see the discussion from the other person's point of view.

As mentioned previously, acknowledgment is a great way to start your discussion. To gain knowledge and understanding from this person, you will need to build trust in order to get them to open up. You have chosen the person you have to be your partner for a reason. Whatever the reason is, acknowledge it. Be sure it is sincere and not over the top. It should be your goal to make them understand how important they are to you.

Another great way to solidify trust and smooth your path forward is to find and discuss common ground. Bring the conversation around to topics where you know you both have common ground.

In my case, my wife and I both had had enough of winter, so it stood to reason we could agree on many things around that topic. The more times she answered yes, the more likely it was she would continue answering yes.

I began to discuss what I had seen the previous week in the marinas I had visited. I asked many questions about whether she would enjoy such a life. I was careful to frame each question in such a way as to cast a positive idea. She has never learned to swim, so I certainly didn't want to plant an idea that might represent threat, such as a boat out in threatening seas.

As you develop such a conversation be interested in the wants and needs of your potential partner. Ask them about the obstacles they face and understand them from their perspective. What may seem like a small obstacle to you might be an insurmountable object to them. Be sure to understand why.

While your research should have developed some assumptions about your prospective partner's wants, weigh them against the reality that has presented itself. Come to understand how this person ranks their wants. What is most important to them? Consider whether the benefits of your plan match their key wants. Be sure that your research doesn't bias your discovery gleaned from your discussions.

If there is disagreement, do not engage in dispute. Rather, show empathy in working to understand their point of view. Diffuse the situation with statements like "I understand how you feel". This removes animosity from the discussion and allows for more open-minded consideration of each other's point of view. Remember that cooperation is best achieved as a result of collaboration. So, be flexible and adaptable. Also remember that a person convinced against their will is not a person convinced. You are far better to use compromise to win over an ally than to use force to create a detractor.

Whose Idea Was This?

To be successful in selling any idea, you need to think like your audience does. In my case, I needed to understand what motivated her and connect my vision to those motivations. As I mentioned she didn't even know how to swim, so "Let's go sailing" was NOT going to resonate with her quite the same as it did with me.

Instead, I started by asking her how her week was. With 20" of snow having fallen over three days, I knew the answer was going to be blunt, but I needed her to say it. When she blurted out, "I'm SO done with winter!" I got exactly what I was hoping for. She had identified a problem that was giving her significant grief and had already gone so far as to lead toward a solution in that she wanted an alternative to winter.

When I asked her, "What does that mean?" she replied, "I love being close to family, but I wish we could go south for the winter".

She was already starting to create a plan, regardless of whether she was serious, that led right into my vision. After prompting her to expand on her thinking she virtually presented my idea as her own without even so much as a mention from me. Of course, this took some subtle discussion about what I saw from that plane window - sailboats floating at anchor. Homes that could be relocated as the weather changed.

But never did I even suggest that I had independently decided to sell everything and buy a boat. In planting the suggestions of others living a life on a boat, she was able to create her own vision of what life would be like if we sold everything and said goodbye to winter. For her, the living on a boat was simply a means to an end. It was a practical way that she could live in warmer climates year-round.

She saw the advantages, colored by her winter-hating glasses, so clearly that they blinded her to any of the challenges or potential obstacles. Suddenly, it seemed almost as if she was asking me if we could/should do this.

Obviously, not every idea that you ever need to sell to make the dream work is going to be this easy. The point, however, is that people are by nature selfish creatures. Whether we admit it consciously or not, our most primary instinct is to ask, "What's in it for me?" whenever anything is asked of us. Unless you live alone on a deserted island, completely detached from society, it's pretty much inevitable that you will need to win partners over to your idea.

Putting your ego aside and letting your partners believe it was originally their idea is a small price to pay to win them over.

Role Play

As you create your vision and begin to develop your plan of execution, consider the roles of each member of your team. Will they be a partner, a contributor, or someone you simply need to be in agreement with enough that they won't seek to sabotage you?

In my case, Leanne was my partner. In life, in starting my business, in going sailing, I needed her to be onside with anything I do, to move forward. That is the foundation of a solid, trusting relationship.

As mentioned, my son was due to finish high school the June before we left so I hoped he would be a partner as well. He had no idea what he wanted to do next, so I proposed that going sailing for a year would be a great way to figure it out. In lieu of a year of college, he would get a year of life lesson.

Our community was bigger than that, though. I had parents, as did Leanne, who we truly hoped would support our unconventional plan. We would need their help in various ways, so it was important to get them to agree to be contributors vs detractors.

Take the time to outline who will be on your team and what role you will ask them to play. Then consider your ask from their point of view. What will motivate them to see your vision as positively as you do? What objections will they bring forward?

Throughout this process, always remember that the goal is not to strong-arm anyone into embracing your vision precisely as you crafted it in your first draft. Instead, your goal should be to present the vision you have, with consideration given to your partner's motivations, concerns, and objectives. In the end, you should seek to create a win/win proposal that satisfies the key points of your vision while also serving the needs of your partner if you wish to gain true collaboration.

With Leanne acknowledging that her life lacked the meaningful purpose she once envisioned, this opened a door of opportunity that led to our deeper discussion. Eventually, she saw the vision as her own and embraced it.

I had been resisting going to her until I had worked out more details. In essence, I wanted to wait to sell her until I had a more complete picture. Instead, I trusted in her ability to dream or at least support my dream. I rationalized that if I knew she was onboard, she would become an important ally in helping me untangle my bias'.

Even with the little detail I could offer, Leanne was a partner almost instantly. While she outlined a lot of holes in the plan which needed discussion, she convinced me that I didn't need to listen only to "Responsible Shawn" any longer. As 'Dreamer Shawn' sprang to life, we ploughed through the mental block that had me convinced there was no more to life than 9-5 to 65.

As we ventured out onto Chesapeake Bay, that plan had become reality, and both Leanne and Daeyten were onboard with it. While I still struggled with doubts at times as to whether we made a responsible decision, I understood the origin of the doubts, and had strategies to silence them.

When we stopped briefly in Norfolk, Virginia, we hooked up with the Sail Magazine Rally group, and our community grew to 18 boats crewed by people who were living their dream. We now had a community of like-minded people who had a vision similar to ours. These were people we could now draw support from.

We left Norfolk on November 1 with a goal to sail together to Miami, hoping to arrive just before Christmas. As it turned out, it was one of the coldest falls on record on the eastern seaboard. So, we quickly learned that sailing wasn't always that ideal life I envisioned from that plane window. Some days were downright hard work. For roughly six weeks, we spent almost everyday waking at first light and sailing until well into the afternoon. With two large dogs onboard, we also had to negotiate ways to get them to shore regularly to take care of business. For much of the trip, we would be out in the elements with as much as seven layers on just to keep hypothermia away. I often said that at times, it was hell! But it was a hell that I would not have traded for the world.

I signed on for the vision of a floating home in a sub-tropical paradise. What I got was so much more! From the history of the Dismal Swamp to the many landscapes we encountered beyond - the Intercoastal Waterway presented an America that you don't see from a plane, or even a car window while driving along an Interstate highway. The collective of the people we met told us a story of what America is really made of. From one small community to the next, we consistently met people living their lives who were thrilled that we had stopped to visit. While many had little to give, they were eager to help us in anyway they could. In Elizabeth City, NC, a greeting party awaited our arrival to take us to wherever we needed to go, to gather whatever provisions we required. In Beaufort, SC, the town hosted a reception for us, followed by a Thanksgiving dinner three days later. In between, we were greeted by more dolphins than I could keep count of!

Along the 1200 nautical mile journey, I realized many firsts as a captain - the most obvious being navigating my first lock, first lift bridge, first fixed bridge, and my first sailing in currents and tides. None of these compared to the opportunity that I was given to experience my wife and my son on a daily basis, taking on these challenges with me. We developed a closeness and cohesiveness that I treasure more than all else.

Compass Point Reflections:

1) Be Engaged
When building partnerships, be interested in their point of view and be empathetic to their concerns.
2) What Do They Want/Need?
Talk in terms of the other person's interest. Know what they want and need, in order to engage their collaboration.
3) Cooperation Beats Confrontation

Cooperation is best achieved through compromise and collaboration.

"Words that soak into your ears are whispered, not yelled." ~ Anonymous

CHAPTER 9 - MAP TO THE SIMPLE LIFE

"Lack of direction, not lack of time, is the problem. We all have twenty-four-hour days." ~ Zig Ziglar

In order to draw a map for yourself, there are two vital pieces of information that you need. First, you need to know where you are, then you need clarity of what your destination is.

As a teenager, I had pledged I would live a simple life. My goal was to experience the things I enjoyed as often as possible, while not over-complicating things. I was certain that wouldn't be too challenging.

What I failed to understand is that most people, myself included, seem to possess a natural instinct to make life complicated. As we experiment with adulting, we get jobs and develop the ability to acquire things. As we do, we convince ourselves we need more. Suddenly, that two-bedroom house isn't big enough and that compact car isn't fancy enough. Before we know it, many of us find ourselves living in a house that we regularly only use a small part of. We fill the house with many things that we use only occasionally, and we drive cars that cost a lot more than the most basic modes of transportation should cost.

We take much deserved pleasure from having luxuries in our life but forget what the cost is to acquire such luxuries. In its simplest element, life is essentially a game of bartering. Unless you were born to wealth, what you barter to acquire things is time. Time is something we're given at birth, but its also something we can't make more of. Sure, if you live your life making healthy decisions, you might stretch your time out, but nothing is guaranteed. So then then the challenge becomes how to make the best use of whatever time we have.

This is where things get complicated. In my life, I determined that in going to college, I would spend time, to get an education. In theory this would make the time that I had to barter more valuable. When I entered the corporate world and started having success, the monetary return on my time increased even more. Unfortunately, as I began to take inventory of what I had acquired from bartering my time, it wasn't as rewarding as I had hoped. We had two cars, two houses, but my sense of purpose was dangerously low.

I remember going on a trip to Dominican Republic and visiting a small fishing village. After having spent the day with the locals we boarded the bus. I recall one person commenting how unfortunate it was how they lived. What I had taken note of was how happy they were. Yes, they lived in small shacks, but they lived seaside. In fact, they generally only used those shacks to sleep in or seek shelter during inclement weather. They got to live 24-7, 365 in a place where I bartered my time to be for only four hours. It was then that I began to rediscover the concept of what I considered a simple life.

Developing our plan to move aboard a sailboat required transition. Five years earlier, Leanne and I each had our own homes. In those five years we had to shed many things to downsize from 2 homes to one. Now we were downsizing from a 1600 square foot home, with a garage, to about 400sq feet total. This is a concept you need to be prepared for. Even for a person who pledged he was ready for a simpler life; this process challenged me at times. I was a sports memorabilia collector. Such things had no place on a boat, but they were still hard to give up.

Through the process of downsizing, we actually made it a rule that we could not take anything with us unless it had at least two purposes. I worried often that asking Leanne to give up 50% of the shoes she had acquired would be the point where reality kicked in and she kicked me to the curb. Fortunately, we both began to see how much stuff we had needlessly collected. As our garage became emptier, our hearts got fuller. We were giving away things we no longer needed and it was as if a burden was being lifted off of us as well.

At this point in my life, Leanne and I have gotten a much clearer picture of what we truly need. Clothes are obviously a necessity because no one wants to see me naked. Beyond that, there's not much. Family is probably next on the list. As far as shelter, our needs are very basic. As long as we have shelter from the elements and the ability to enjoy the elements when the weather allows we're happy. Making the tough choices we made when we went sailing taught us that purpose and fulfillment aren't tied to possessions. These things are connected to experience.

As you stake out your dream life, take a good look at your surroundings. Be honest with yourself in determining what you truly need, vs what you've convinced yourself you need. In considering something's value to you, consider how much time is sacrificed on it vs how much happiness it brings. Think about how much is truly lost in a life without that thing. Then ask yourself if it separates you or brings you closer to your vision of a dream life. Remember to only measure these things using your values. Don't let society's values mess up your judgement.

Dead Reckoning…Determine Your True Position

The challenge we often face in determining where we are can be a struggle. Often times, we find it hard to be honest with ourselves about where we are in life. Have you ever said, "everything is fine" when deep down, you knew that it wasn't? A basic human trait is to convince ourselves that we are exactly where we ought to be, exactly where we planned to be, even when its clear we're not.

There are many reasons why we tend to hide the truth, some of which can be deeply rooted in sub-conscious behaviors, even connected back to childhood. There are also some common reasons that dwell much closer to the surface.

1) Change Avoidance

One such reason we tend to avoid being honest is because we know change can be difficult and perhaps scary. We rationalize that if we admit things aren't perfect, then we need to do something about it. Suddenly, we'll be compelled to step outside our comfort zone and chart a course through unknown territory.

2) Fear of Failure

Fear of failure, and/or a fear of being seen as a failure is another reason that we convince ourselves that everything is fine. Imagine, for example, that you have risen to the level of supervisor at your place of employment. If you admit to someone that you aspire to be a manager, suddenly, you might wonder if they see you as a failure in that you have not achieved that level yet. Or perhaps you fear they will see you that way if you don't rise to that level soon enough?

I worked hard to convince myself that I was exactly where I wanted to be perhaps because I feared that admitting things weren't perfect somehow diminished the many accomplishments I took pride in.

I had a good job, and I was newly married to my long-lost childhood crush. Business was going extremely well, and I had built many solid business relationships. I rationalized what could possibly be wrong with my life?

These blinders prevented me from seeing that I had gotten stuck in such a way that my Career pillar was flourishing at the expense of my Self and Family/Community pillars. The result was it was eroding my overall health and happiness and jeopardizing my enduring success.

When the new VP came along and seemed determined to discount the success my team was having in growing our business, it exposed the lack of balance in my life. It highlighted the fact that my success was one dimensional. In relation to the other two pillars, I suddenly developed a sense that I was failing.

As you define your position, remember that this is a process that does not need to include anyone else. Taking stock on your own enables you to be far more honest with yourself. At the start of this book, I suggested you acquire a notebook as your study aid. This is a great example for its use as a private journal of your thoughts. Document where you perceive yourself, and how it makes you feel. Go back a day or a week later and consider if they were your truest feelings and become curious about why you think you feel that way. What are you trying to tell yourself?

As you become more comfortable with your feelings, consider the value that could come to the process if you brought in a trusted confident to discuss these feelings. This should be someone who's goal is not to influence your perceptions but to help facilitate your self evaluation. If you really struggle in this area, remember that there are coaches, therapists and support groups that are available for support. Also, remember that you are not the only person who gets caught in this trap. When you walk down any street, it's more likely than not that over half the people you see have encountered the fear of failure or will, in their lifetime.

Where Do You Want to Be?

Once you define your position in life with clarity, an equally daunting task still lies ahead. Defining where you want to be can easily be colored by false filters. We often seek out artificial desires to define what we wish to get from our lives. Simple markers can include a bigger house, increased salary, or fancy title. Be sure to reflect back on your passion and dreams statements to be sure you clearly articulate your desired destination.

When I reached this point, I opened my laptop and immediately began to pen a letter to myself. I dated it one year ahead and detailed what my life was like then after having made the changes detailed in my vision. I made the vision come to life in this letter to shift the perspective from "one day I will" to "I did, and this is what it looks like".

In the forward dated letter, I described the boat I purchased and talked about where we've been, and where we were headed. This became the destination that I used to draw my roadmap and shape my plan. It gave me the permission and confidence to buy into that plan.

Imagine trying to use a map if you have yet to define your destination and bring clarity to it. In going through this process, you will get a very clear picture of where you want to be. It will be a picture of where you WILL be in the future.

Once I had my wife to the point where she had adopted my vision as her own and was open to it in principle, I showed her my letter in order to clearly articulate how and why we should change our lives.

It took only moments before she hugged me and said thank you before a tear rolled down her cheek. I reeled in horror as I pondered "Did I just give her the reason she needed for leaving me?".

Fact was, she was also stuck, and my letter saved her from creating her own vision and gave her the wake-up call she too needed. We were exactly on the same page, and that was a tear of joy for rescuing her! GAME ON!

I had spent so many years of my life living almost entirely under my "Responsible Shawn" persona I feared "Dreamer Shawn" was suffocating. Suddenly, the two were collaborating peacefully. While Headshaker was still making noise, the other two personas were drowning him out. It was marvelous!

Compass Point Reflections:

1) Write Your Own Story

As you reflect on how you want to change your life, don't be afraid to shut the world out of the process. This is YOUR story, not theirs. While there will be stakeholders in your network who you will count on for support, contribution, and possibly partnership, the time to include them will come later. Right now, this is about you and you alone. Enjoy this moment! Be Bold. In writing your story, come at it from the point of view that it can be exactly whatever you want it to be. Now is not the time to consider anything but the best life you can envision. There is absolutely no place for the

Headshaker to be involved in this moment, and little need to involve Responsible Self. Give Dreamer Self unlimited freedom to create a vision that captures all that you could ask for.

2) Write your letter to self

Capture your story in a letter to yourself. Date the letter one year ahead in order to move you from 'one day' to active mode. Be definitive and detailed about what your life looks like one year down the road once you have executed the plan you will create. This letter should be about creating your future reality so you can develop the plan to get there. The one year criteria is not set in stone, but don't extend it out too long.

"When everything is coming your way, you're in the wrong lane." ~ Anonymous

CHAPTER 10 - SEE BEYOND THE HORIZON

"The visionary starts with a clean sheet of paper and re-imagines the world." ~ Malcolm Gladwell

Many people live their lives with far too little awareness of how much potential they have to be in control of their own destiny. Imagine it's like they're riding on a bus - they pay the fare and hope the bus will take them where they want to go. The problem is that many don't even know where they want to go, let alone how to get there.

There was a point in my life, where I was living like that. I got married at twenty-five and became a father not long after. When that happened, I set aside virtually all the dreams I had for my future and turned my focus to becoming a provider. I lived day to day, hoping I could simply feed my family and see my kids grow up. I paid little attention to the most important pillar of a balanced life: Self. The result was it negatively affected all three pillars.

That day when I looked out the plane window, at sailboats forming floating communities it gave me cause to take stock of where I was. It was then that I realized my life looked nothing like the life I had imagined as a youth and young adult. When I was younger, I was a visionary. Nothing was too ambitious for me. I believed I was destined for great things - Prime Minister, NHL coach? There were no limits to my imagination. Somehow, I let the Headshaker and Responsible Self kidnap the visionary and lock him away. I found myself asking "How do I get the visionary back?". The fact is, being a visionary is a choice that we all can make. There is a set of learned behaviors that we can adopt to become visionaries. Once we become intentional about adopting these behaviors, the world changes. What once seemed impossible will become routine. You will start to see that ambitions are no longer unreachable but rather a good plan away from realization.

You may be skeptical, so let me first tell you about the rest of our adventure. In total we sailed approximately 2500 nautical miles from Annapolis, MD to the Florida Keys, and back to Toronto, Ontario, Canada. While experienced sailors might be exclaiming "big whoop!" as I've stated we were anything but experienced sailors. We simply figured it out and got lucky. We spent 13 months living aboard, before expanding our vision, and then expanding it again. You see, after we lived the sailing life, our curiosity of the world grew. We determined that seeing the world by boat was exciting, but it was also a slow process. So in the summer of 2016 we developed a plan to see a bit more of the world by purchasing a motorhome.

On December 1, 2015, we left Ontario and headed for Mexico. After a brief stop in Corpus Christi, Texas, we crossed the border into Mexico on December 18. Determined to make it to Playa Del Carmen by Christmas, we drove three long days, stopping at Mexican gas stations to park for the night. While we found it strange that the first gas station was visited by a rotation of police officers throughout the night, we found out the next morning that it was because the station was robbed at gunpoint the night previous to our stay. The following night, we stopped in the small coastal town of Tampico and parked right in the centre of town. This is where we learned that our two Alaskan Malamutes terrified the locals - so much so, that NO one wanted anything to do with us. From that night onward, we were sure to take the dogs for a long walk around the neighbourhoods that we stopped in, being sure to let all the locals know who their guests were. On the last night of our race to Playa Del Carmen, we decided we would splurge by paying to stay in a campground that was listed in the book *Mexican Camping*. The park was in

Merida, and the directions specifically stated "Do NOT go through downtown Merida if you have a big rig, as the streets are too narrow for big rigs". Sadly, our map program didn't take the size of our rig into account as it routed us right through the heart of downtown!

Nonetheless, we persevered, only to get to the campground and discover it was closed! Turned out that it had been sold to developers, then the deal fell through. We were able to call the owners, and they agreed to let us camp there anyway. They advised where to find a key for the gate and advised they would come by later to collect a fee. We had the place to ourselves, the dogs had room to run, there was running water, and a shopping mall right next door. Life was good!

A day later we were in Playa Del Carmen, and we parked at a small campground at a place called Playa Xpu Ha. There were about 10 camping spots located beach side with a beach club beside us. By day, it was a popular spot for tourists to get away from their resorts to listen to a chorus of waves and local musicians, while they sipped on their libation of choice and dipped in turquoise waters. By night, it became "total tranquilo," as the sun dipped into the sea.

We spent about three months there while Leanne took her yoga teacher training. Once she completed it, we headed as far south as the Belize border before backtracking north, then west, to the other coast. Eventually we made our way north again, in time to stop in Las Vegas for the National Hardware Show. As much as we were adventuring, I was still running a business.

Our first adventure, going sailing, took an enormous amount of energy and courage. Having succeeded without dying developed a confidence in us that fed off of itself. As we planned our sailing adventure, well into it I would wake up at times in a sweat, questioning if I had lost my mind. "This is not what you're supposed to do!" I would think to myself.

For the next adventures, it came naturally. It became the new normal. It brought the visionary back, and I was comfortable with it! Luckily, the visionary was no longer determined to become prime minister or something equally thankless. My new visionary simply was determined to live life without limits that bound me to meeting society's definition of a "normal life". That allowed us to become so comfortable that we went on to a third adventure that I can't wait to tell you about - but let's talk about becoming a visionary first.

In order for me to become a visionary again, there were some behaviors I had to check at the door, and some new ones I had to learn. The most obvious was that I had gotten too serious about life. My inability to shut down was indicative of that. As I've mentioned, it seemed like I thought I was saving the world. I wasn't. That was the first thing I had to learn. Then I began to adopt these behaviors.

Eight Habits of a Visionary

Be Confident but Humble - No matter what it is that you determine you want from life, confidence is a critical ingredient to your success. Show me anyone who has ever achieved greatness in their life, and I'll show you a person who started out by believing in themselves. Confidence doesn't come naturally, and it can't be faked. Confidence comes from learning to build a plan for success that is thought out, researched, and considers as many possibilities as can be imagined. Almost every year, in virtually every pro sport, you see at least one team that was a favorite but got beaten by an underdog. While injuries and other uncontrollable circumstances are typically a part of such upsets, the other undeniable truth is that the underdog went into the competition with a plan, and the player or players bought into the plan. That gave them the confidence to look beyond stats and believe success was possible.

The other side of that coin is Be Humble. Underdogs are typically most successful when they go about their work dutifully and in unassuming fashion. After almost every upset victory, it's almost inevitable that you see a coach in front of the media being asked how they did it. Almost always, you'll hear the coach reply modestly such as "We simply wanted it more". This is a moment where the coach could talk about how he predicted every move the opponent would make and devised a masterful counter. He could talk about how he achieved loyalty from his players, facilitated the execution of the plan, and made failure impossible. Such insolence serves no purpose other than to motivate those who wish to defeat you.

When you are humble, it creates followers. How many times have you watched a humble underdog take the high road and find yourself hoping that they win it all? Being confident yet humble in your own life has the same effect. People will start to not only believe in you, but they'll also become your greatest fans. When this happens, you'll build a support network that will help pave your road to success.

Live In Curiosity - Until recently, I thought I needed to have all the answers to be successful. Ironically, my success came as a result of being very curious in my younger years. When I started out in sales, I worked for a manufacturer's agent, where I represented several manufactured product lines, selling to retailers and industrial distributors. In essence, I had several bosses, including the owner and general manager of our company, as well as dotted line bosses being the sales manager of the companies we represented. I used these many relationships to sponge up as much knowledge as I could. Having this many mentors meant that I could learn the secrets to their success and build an approach that was the culmination of all their secrets. My curiosity and willingness to learn enabled me to do this.

When I became a sales manager, I misinterpreted the rules of engagement, believing that I suddenly had to be the man who had all the answers. In February of 2023, I signed up for an Executive Leadership Coach course where I discovered that a true leader lives in curiosity and relies on those around him/her to satisfy that curiosity. I discovered that I will never be an expert in other people's lives. As a leader, I now realize that my role is to discover what challenges and opportunities others face and facilitate the discovery of their own solutions.

Using that philosophy on our boat while we were sailing could have been extremely more productive. For example, Daeyten, my son, and I had many disagreements. Trying to dock in Elizabeth City is one that comes to mind. He had a theory on how to be successful, as did I. Unfortunately, I thought it was my role as leader, or captain, to know how to dock, so I failed to listen to his ideas. What's worse is that I failed to understand why his ideas were important to him. The result was that we cast the outward perception to what seemed like the whole town, that we were a circus of grossly inexperienced sailors who despised each other, as we failed several attempts to land safely. Reflecting back now, I consider that Daeyten was a smart young man capable of conceiving valid, workable methods to dock successfully. What likely was most important to him in that moment was to be recognized as such in being heard. Had I given him that, there would have been no obligation to adopt everything just as he proposed; merely hear it and consider it. If I felt that his ideas were not best suited to my skills or perceptions of the surrounding circumstances all I had to do is explain that respectfully. Its far more likely that we would have understood and cooperated with each other in a more productive fashion then.

Be Accountable to Self - To be a true visionary, you must embrace the notion that you are accountable for your own success. In life, we have two types of experiences - the moments when we achieve the result we expect and moments that become learning opportunities.

Visionaries take note of why they were successful as much as they take note of why they weren't and then use these observations as a tool for creating a process for future successes. For a visionary, success does not happen by chance. Rather, success happens on purpose, drawn from a detailed and well-executed plan.

An import thing to note here is that success breeds success. As outlined previously in this chapter, when we were successful in pursuing our sailing adventure, it built the confidence to pursue our next adventure. In order to maximize this effect, you must be intentional about recognizing the success, and recognizing your role in the success, just as you must recognize your role as they relate to opportunities to learn and improve.

Visualize Your Desired Outcome - Success is most easily achieved after you gain a clear understanding of what success looks like. High-level athletes do this by playing the game in their minds long before they ever take to the field. They create a clear image of what success is to them, then imagine themselves executing the success in detail. You too should make this regular practice. Define for yourself what the greatest outcomes possible are, and then convince yourself that they are entirely within your control by visualizing them coming to reality.

When we went sailing, I had imagined leaving port and sailing south hundreds of times long before I even had a boat. By the time we arrived in Florida, I had visualized that reality so often that it was almost anti-climatic - ALMOST. This gave me the confidence to get through many challenges and moments of adversity. In essence, I had convinced myself that the conclusion I hoped for was already set in stone, and I simply had to perform the steps that were pre-determined to afford success. It was kind of like watching a movie that I had already seen - I knew the outcome.

Of course, I cautioned myself to be prepared for unexpected moments of adversity. However, playing out many scenarios in my head and always allowing myself to imagine the same final conclusion enabled me to challenge adversity with greater confidence and determination.

Set Goals - As incredible as it may sound, as many as 80% of the population lives their lives without ever setting goals. What's even worse is of the ones who do, only a small minority ever see their goals through to fruition.

Goals are one of many tools that keep people moving forward. While I have emphasized the importance of recognizing and acknowledging success, goals serve as a means of reminding you that there are next steps. This reduces the likelihood of complacency, that could cause you to get stuck.

In my life, I had sketched out a rough guideline of what I hoped to accomplish in my career, but failed to fill out the other boxes, so to speak. Once I achieved that which I set out to achieve in my career, and neglected to update my goals, or expand them, I found myself stuck.

Effective goal setting is achieved when you establish a clear vision of your destination, outline a set of steps/goals that align with that vision, and then detail a process or plan that will take you from your current place to that intended destination. Remember that your goals statement must always be a living document, which is updated regularly, based on the progress you make.

Dare to Act - The world is full of great intentions. Unfortunately, many people stop at intentions. Ask yourself if you've ever heard someone say "one day" when talking about buying a boat, or taking a dream vacation, or doing something extraordinary?

After we went sailing, we heard many people use that term as we discussed our journey and they compared it to their dream.

Sadly, I know far too many people who left this world far too soon, long before "one day" arrived for them. Please don't let that happen to you.

As discussed in previous chapters, we tend to say "I should" when discussing something we aspire to do. That puts it in a realm of possibility, without any commitment. Make a commitment by moving from "one day" or "I should" to "I am". Make it active and commit to it.

Pop quiz - Are you ready? Correct answer: "I AM".

Be Honest with Yourself - An important part of daring to act is being honest with yourself about how far you are prepared to go and what sacrifices you are prepared to make.

Most, if not all of us, aspire to great things in life. Sadly, we often convince ourselves that those things are out of reach for reasons beyond our control. But is this true?

Suppose you are twenty-five years old, and you want to retire at fifty-five years old. Now beware, I am NOT a certified financial planner, so take this with a grain of salt. Imagine you start investing $500 per month and increase those contributions by the rate of inflation each year. Assuming you realize an average return of 10% per year, you will have approximately $1 million by age fifty-five. So, then the question becomes, are you committed to making the sacrifice of investing that amount every month?

If your goal is to become Senior VP in five years, it will take a lot of work to get there. You will also need to ensure that you use the Three Pillars of a Balanced Life to avoid sacrificing your health of Self, and Family/Community. Are you prepared to maintain that balance?

The key here is that whatever constitutes a dream life for you, chances are some sacrifices will be involved in realizing that life. It's easy to say that you are prepared for the sacrifice, but its harder to live up to it. Make sure you understand what sacrifices you will need to make and be honest with yourself when committing to them. If your willingness to sacrifice causes you to come up short of your goal, know this sooner rather than later to enable you to adjust your goals to realize a revised success.

As we headed south on *Suenos*, our sailboat, I pondered the honesty question many times. I love being on the water but the unknown of the depths also terrified me. I asked myself many times how I would react if/when we got out of sight of shore. It was a challenge I felt I was up for - or hoped! I was prepared for the possibility that we might have needed to revise our vision of success.

Focus On What's Important to You - Through this process, your priorities must remain at the forefront. As we've discussed previously, we are programmed to believe narratives that don't align with what we truly want from life. As you read these words, I want you to become intentional about living a life that is focused on your priorities. The Three Pillars of a Balanced Life challenge you to consider Career, and Family, as well as Self. Understand that an intense focus on Self, and the priorities you consider most important, will not only serve the Self pillar. In working intentionally to serve the Self pillar, and creating a healthier YOU, you will also become far better equipped to serve the other two pillars.

We heard of many people who thought we were crazy. Not for daring to dream, but for daring to pursue our dream. We thought it crazy to NOT pursue our dream.

Do not let the values or expectations of judgmental society sidetrack your vision. Stay true to yourself.

.

Compass Point Reflections:

1) Embrace, adopt and live by The Eight Habits to Become A Visionary:
    - Be confident but humble.
    - Live in curiosity.
    - Be accountable to Self.
    - Visualize your desired outcome.
    - Set goals.
    - Dare to act.
    - Be honest with yourself.
    - Focus on what's important to you.

"Visionary people face the same problems everyone else faces; but rather than get paralyzed by their problems, visionaries immediately commit themselves to finding a solution." ~ Bill Hybels

CHAPTER 11 - CHART CONVICTION

"Setting goals is the first step in turning the invisible into the visible." ~ Tony Robbins

I am an avid believer in goal setting. When I look back at my life, I can classify the various eras into one of two different categories. On the one side there would be the times when I was living on the rumble strip, happy to accept what life presented me, and on the other side, the times when I took an active role in my destiny. Whenever I was taking an active role, I had a vision, a clear set of goals, and a plan to achieve those goals. I am sure you can imagine which eras brought me more happiness. Think of your goals as your chart, or map. While they must be flexible to changing circumstances be convicted to them.

With every step of our sailing adventure, I always had several goals lying ahead of me. As one goal was checked off, I was always sure to assess where that got me and bring myself to understand what new objectives that brought into focus. Long before we arrived back in Toronto aboard *Suenos*, I was already assessing what our plan was for the following winter and building goals accordingly. When we decided we would RV through Mexico, there was still the possibility it might not come to fruition, so I planned two sets of goals. One set had us sailing back south come fall. One set of goals was dependent on the outcome of research about RVing in Mexico.

As we discussed in previous chapters, a key ingredient of success is having clarity in your vision. Knowing where you want to be is important. Developing a plan to get you there is the next step, but still only the beginning. If you said you wanted to own your own successful fashion business within five years, that would be the vision. A plan would be something like outlining that you will get a job in the industry, build all the right contacts, and collect the necessary resources, including financial.

Still, you would need to break the plan into several smaller, more detailed, actionable steps that are commonly referred to as goals. This is the recipe or "how" of your plan.

In our case, when we said we wanted to go sailing, that was the vision. What followed was a long series of detailed and actionable steps that addressed "how" would I find myself on a boat, sailing to sunny climates?

What is important is that you break things down into small bite-size pieces that, if executed properly, will advance you toward successful execution of your plan. Be sure that you define your goals with criteria that will enable you to measure your progress.

Remember that the goal-setting process is much like a recipe; that a recipe has two components- ingredients and directions on what to do with the ingredients. If you follow the recipe correctly, it should deliver you to your destination.

Goal Setting Roadblocks

As incredible as it may sound, only about 20% of us set goals on a regular basis, and of the 20%, many fail to fully follow through on the goals they set. Understanding the why of this can help you avoid the same destiny. Here is a breakdown of some of the most common reasons why so many fail to execute their goals:

Lack of Destination - The first step in goal setting, which we've already discussed, is defining your destination, or defining clearly what you seek from life and why you are setting goals in the first place. This can also include being too vague in defining your destination. If you don't clearly define where you want to be, you will find it very difficult to create specific goals and a detailed plan to get you there.

Failure to Follow Up - Often, what happens is people fail to fully understand the goal setting process. They define their destination and write beautiful goals that truly capture the essence of their vision, then set them aside, expecting them to happen spontaneously. They fail to recognize that setting the goal is merely the first step of the process. Then you must define what is the measurement that indicates successful completion. Finally, you must set deadlines for goal completion, and hold yourself accountable to that deadline and then take action.

Fear - As we've already discussed fear is a very real limiter to successful goal completion and perhaps one of the most potentially dangerous limiters. Take that first step.

Am I Worthy Mindset - We are conditioned to believe that an extraordinary life is not something we are entitled to. If you find yourself caught in that way of thinking, consider one simple question: "Why NOT me?"

Over Thinking It - Another tendency people get caught in is over-thinking. They detail the destination, set the goals, detail a plan, and then start to sweat the details. While it's important to have a well thought out plan with contingencies don't get caught in an endless spiral of overthinking it! A key part of success is knowing when you've planned enough, and when its time to start executing. The key isn't to have the perfect plan - its to have an adaptive mindset and trust yourself!

Be prepared to shift your focus when the situation warrants it. Don't mire endlessly on one task if you are stuck. Shift your focus elsewhere, and you'll find that when you come back to that task, you are likely to come back with a new perspective that will ease your path.

This strategy can also be effective when confronted with an obstacle beyond your control that will delay completion. To stay on track as best as possible, consider what other items you can work on while that obstacle sorts itself out.

The MOST important part of goal setting that I challenge you to consider is to maintain balance. As you set your goals, always think about how each goal serves the Three

Pillars of A Balanced Life and gets you closer to realizing your vision for a dream life.

Compass Point Reflections:

1) Measure The Execution

Don't forget to assign measurable criteria, or Key Performance Indicators (KPI's), to determine when each step or goal is complete. Set target dates for completion of every goal.

2) Be flexible

Use deadlines as guidelines - not set in stone. Inevitably, you will encounter unexpected obstacles, which are impossible to plan for. Flexibility will allow you to adapt without getting discouraged.

"What you get by achieving your goals is not as important as what you become by achieving your goals."
~ Zig Ziglar

CHAPTER 12 – STAY THE COURSE

"A hero is an ordinary individual who finds the strength to persevere and endure in spite of overwhelming obstacles." ~ Christopher Reeve

When we arrived home from our RV adventure, we were faced with a dilemma. In running a business in Canada, while spending so much time abroad, it seemed like I was living with one foot in and one foot out. Leanne did the accounting for the business, which was easy to do from wherever we were. For me, I always had to be connected and close to an airport. I was spending about 40% of my time away from my family, travelling on business. In a sense, it seemed very similar to the corporate life - just without a safety net. It was time to go all in or get out.

We found ourselves at a point where we felt we were too young to retire but too independent to return to corporate life.

Essentially, we resolved to stay the course we had set, a life of adventure. But now we needed to replace the income I'd be giving up in ridding us of the Canadian business. So we began to search for ways to give up our Canadian business and earn an income abroad that connected better with who we had become. One day a boat neighbor came to us and asked if we had ever heard of Roatan? He proceeded to tell us about this small Honduran island, 40 miles off the mainland, which was a scuba diving mecca. Then he showed us a beachside bar that was for sale. Our wheels started turning, as I began to dig deeper. A few days later, another person told us about friends of theirs who had a catamaran business for sale in Roatan. At that point, we decided it warranted a trip there to investigate. Long story short, neither opportunity was right for us, but we also looked at an old three-story wood apartment building that was for sale. It had seen better days and was badly in need of a makeover. But it sat on a third of an acre, sitting hillside, with a jungle backdrop overlooking the Caribbean Sea. We could turn three apartments into five and make it a vacationer's jungle retreat. We were sold.

We took possession of the property on November 1, 2016. Leanne stayed in Ontario, waiting until a window opened to get the dogs down there mid November. So, it was Daeyten and I who went ahead to complete the paperwork and take possession. Until then, we had not seen all areas of the building, and that which we did see was merely a quick glance. Daeyten had no idea what we were in for.

November is rainy season in Roatan, and this day was eager to prove that. As we crossed the bridge walkway that led us to the building, the creek roared at us. Climbing the many stairs, we had to navigate cautiously as they were rain soaked and treacherous. We went to the top floor first. When opening the door Daeyten gulped. As we ventured in, we saw a building in need of far more TLC than I remembered. Next was the middle floor, then the bottom floor.

After finishing our inspection, Daeyten asked "Dad, what did you do?".

"Its not that bad" came my reply, though I wasn't convinced. Nonetheless, we set about the task of demolition, knowing that much had to go before we could create the vision that would eventually become the "Jungle Reef Inn".

After a few days we had the demolition done, and it was time to develop a plan to rebuild. Rebuilding is something I had done back in Canada on numerous projects. What I didn't consider was that now I was in a foreign country where the first language was Spanish. I knew enough Spanish to order a beer or find a bathroom, but hardly enough to order building materials or hire contractors. So here we were, with an old building, torn apart, that had to be put back together before we could earn any income off of it. I was stuck, and I had a lot to figure out.

I recall vividly the phone conversation I had with Leanne that night. I was nearly broken. I had become overwhelmed with trying to determine how to proceed. In Canada, I could walk into a big box hardware store and visually see what building materials were available. I would make design choices accordingly. If I needed help from an employee, there was no language barrier. These conditions did not exist in Roatan - or so I had assumed. If there was a point at which I was prepared to quit, this would have been it.

Leanne listened to my concerns quietly and attentively. Once I was finished spilling every detail of a very frustrating day, she asked, "Do you believe we made a mistake?".

It was a fight or flight moment. I knew there would be challenges. We had already dealt with many challenges in our adventures. I compared that moment to when we discovered we had a cracked mast on our sailboat, which was also very stressful for me. With the cracked mast, our insurance company stepped up and covered the damages, which resolved the situation very admirably.

I replied to Leanne, "NO, we have not made a mistake, I'll figure this out".

Leanne knew that I needed to vent. She knew that I felt alone, and that listening to me would remind me we were in it together. She also knew I would ultimately resolve to stay the course.

Maintain The Rhumb Line

In sailing, the term "Rhumb Line" refers to an imaginary line running directly from two points - typically your departure point and destination if it's a straight course.

However, the challenge in sailing is that we can't control the wind, meaning it doesn't always blow in the ideal direction. This often makes it impossible for you to stay on the rhumb line the whole way. Sometimes, you need to make a series of tacks or jibes (turns in layman terms) back and forth across the rhumb line in order to steer to your destination. This is all dependent on what the wind has in store for you.

The overriding objective is to stay as close as possible to the rhumb line, in order to minimize the time and effort required to reach your destination.

Life is like that as well. As I've mentioned many times, you will encounter obstacles or adversity that is beyond your control. Your ability to adapt and stay as true as possible to your rhumb line will significantly influence your level and rate of success.

This speaks to the importance of being prepared for adversity to the extent of having options built into your plan. In life, there are many variables that we have little or no control over.

We certainly experienced that while sailing. As we worked our way down Chesapeake Bay from Annapolis, MD to Norfolk, VA, we encountered at least a few days of unsettled weather. I had to get to Norfolk to catch a flight back to Toronto for a business meeting. Two days before my flight, a small craft warning was issued for the bay. Rather than consider alternatives, I chose to head out onto the bay to put some more miles behind us. We were two easy days away from Norfolk or one very long day. I figured if we broke it up, we could tolerate some rough weather in smaller chunks.

When we entered onto the bay from the Patuxent River, we were met with big swells ranging between 6-10 feet. My son instantly cited his objection to my decision, while Leanne quietly objected as soon as asked. I quickly decided an alternative was necessary, but as I altered course back toward safety, a large chop pounded us on the starboard side, nearly pushing us right over. It took only minutes to get back to the relative safety of Solomons Island - but they were quiet minutes.

We found a slip to park the boat for a few nights, and I booked a rental car to get me to the airport. As I reflected on the choice I had made, I realized it was made from stubbornness and impatience. My alternate arrangements were made within ten minutes and cost a little more than what our original plan was going to cost.

The difference was that the cost of my stubbornness could have been much higher. I was so determined to stay true to my rhumb line that I risked all of our safety. As bad as that was, my son's response to my choices is what hurt the most. Upon arriving safely back to the marina, he immediately blurted out, "Dad, that's it, I'm going home! I'm done with sailing!".

I was destroyed! We were only three days into this trip that I hoped would shape his life and bond us in a way that few father/sons ever get to share. Now, because of my stubbornness, I had to ruin it! All because I refused to understand the need for flexibility.

See It from Your Team's Eyes

At that moment, I had two choices. As I desperately tried to gather the words of how to respond to my son's demands to go home, it occurred to me that it wasn't my decision to make. He was eighteen, and he was determined. If I were to puff my chest out and declare that Father knows best I would have lost him.

Instead, I looked at him with understanding, remorse, and humility. I declared that I screwed up. Then I told him that I understood why he felt the way he did. I didn't limit my understanding to the fear he felt while on the water. I worked to understand every emotion he was feeling. He was eighteen and wanted to be treated like the young man he had become. In ignoring his objections about going sailing that day, I violated his trust.

In the end, we came to an agreement. From that moment forward, we agreed to what I should have already agreed to. I agreed that I would hear his and Leanne's voices and never over-rule them where safety was concerned. I also agreed that I would give him the recognition that he sought.

He agreed to continue on the journey with us.

In whatever vision you pursue, you will encounter people who see things differently. Their refusal to accept the vision you present isn't always a firm no and it's rarely personal. Often, what it is, is an invitation to address their concerns. What is required is that you take the time to understand what is behind the no and consider how they see things. Ask yourself, if you were them, what would you need to turn a no into a yes, given the understanding of their concern that you gain from curiosity?

That is when you will often find common ground, provided you can be generous enough to afford them flexibility in your plan! This flexibility might mean having to deviate from the rhumb line, but with a good compass and solid navigation, you will determine a way to get back to the rhumb line and maintain your course.

Know The Pitfalls

By now, I'm certain you have a keen understanding of how important options and flexibility are when you create a plan. In sailing, they say, "Never sail on a schedule". They say this for a reason, and I discovered that reason on the day I sailed out of Soloman's Island into rough, choppy waters that triggered the small craft warning.

Fortunately, I learned a lesson that day. The lesson taught me to always plan out my route and consider possible bailouts in case they were needed. If I planned to sail from

A-D, points B and C would be places I could tuck into if necessary. I would also consider things like what I would do if I lost power, or the boat developed a leak. We practice fire drills in school, rarely ever expecting them to be required in real life. But aren't we far better off to be prepared for a moment that might never happen than to be unprepared for any reasonable possibility? That is an investment of time that almost surely will pay off in the increased confidence you will garner, knowing that you are prepared for virtually every foreseeable possibility. In the game of life, confidence is avaluable currency.

Think Outside the Triangle

As we headed back north, we navigated the Gulf of Mexico, from Marathon, FL, to Fort Myers Beach, before turning into and crossing the Okeechobee Waterway. The Okeechobee represented four days of relatively uneventful "sailing". Essentially, this is a straight canal with little opportunity for danger. Other than two lift locks, Lake Okeechobee was the only serious threat, but only if the wind was to kick up. Being a shallow lake, a heavy wind could create big waves, close together, making for a bumpy ride.

The only other piece of significance was a train bridge located just east of the eastern lock. The bridge raised to 49', and our mast was 52'. If you're good at math, I'm sure you're wondering how we pulled that off? Fortunately, a fellow affectionately known as "Billy the Tipper" had a plan to help us to resolve the bridge challenge. When a sailboat is tipped over, it brings the top of mast closer to the water. Picture a triangle formed by the water, the mast and an imaginary line running from the top of the mast to the water. Billy strung a measuring line from the top of the mast to the water that was 47'. The challenge then became for him to tip the boat enough that the line touched the water. To do this, he placed four rain barrels on our port side deck and filled them with water, causing the boat to lean. Hence, *Out of the Triangle* thinking.

Whatever it is that you tackle in pursuit of your dream life, you will inevitably encounter your *49' train bridge*. We've discussed many strategies about how to overcome adversity and continue on. Don't forget the power of thinking *outside the triangle*.

Dead Reckoning

While I've touched on this point a few times, I don't think it can be emphasized enough. In sailing, dead reckoning is the process of pinpointing your location. As circumstances push you off course or slow you down, regularly assessing your position alerts you when it's time to adjust course or consider if you are ahead or behind schedule.

After you take the time to build a detailed plan and outline detailed goals to help you navigate that plan, your efforts will be wasted if you don't take the time to track your progress and know where you are.

Think of your plan as your destination on a map and your stated goals as key landmarks to look for along the way. If you don't continuously track where you are, how will you know that you've completed a goal or stage of the journey indicating it's time to move on to the next stage or goal?

Live Your Story

As you navigate your journey, you will meet forces that will attempt to alter your course. While flexibility is a key component of success, it's equally important that you stay true to who you are and what your vision is. Keep in mind that there is a difference between staying true and being rigid.

When I said I was going to quit my corporate job and start my own business, there were doubters. A year later, when I told people we were going to sell everything, buy a boat and go sailing, the doubter crowd got larger. But we stayed true to our plan. We tweaked the plan as necessary, but never did we allow our plan to be hijacked by people who lacked the perspective we had to understand what we were setting out to do.

Remember, it's always helpful to get opinions and points of view from members of your community whom you trust to have your best interest at stake. But in the end, this is your story, so keep it that way.

The day after my near melting point in Roatan, I called Mike Carter, my real estate agent. It wasn't to re-list the property that I had just torn apart, but rather to elicit some assistance. I resolved that I was going to need a resource that I could lean on to help me get acquainted with the way to get things done there.

First and foremost, I needed to learn where to go for what, and who could speak my language when I got there. I also needed to build a rolodex of contractors that I could seek help from as needed. By the end of the day I had two guys turn our overgrown jungle into something closely resembling a manicured estate. Tyrone not only supplied that labor, but he also took me on a tour of a number of building supply stores, introducing me to people I could utilize to buy just about everything I would need, from lumber to light fixtures, and beyond. Having begun this project on November 1, we were on a very tight timeline. We pledged that we wanted to be open for Christmas. People who had become accustomed to the laid-back lifestyle that is Roatan, often joked "Christmas of what year?".

We received our first guests on December 23, 2016… just shy of 8 weeks after we began demolition. In our renovation, we completely gutted two of the three floors, converted from three apartments to five, added three new bathrooms, a new kitchen, kitchenette, and had fun doing it. Our first guests were three backpackers from Greece, England, and Australia. Their original plan was to use our place as a base to see Roatan. Once they arrived, they didn't leave until three days later, when they were scheduled to check out. They said they loved the place so much, there was no place they wanted to be more. Guess we did something right?

Compass Point Reflections:

1) Bend but Don't Break

There's a saying *"anything worth doing is never easy"*. You will be pushed and pulled. Keep your eyes on the destination, and when you're pulled off course, trust your compass to guide you back.

2) Think Outside the Box

Or outside the triangle! Tough tasks will often require creative thinking. Rise to the challenge - or call *Billy the Tipper*!

3) Your Story

It's your story - don't invite people into it who don't have your interest at heart, and don't let others write your story.

> *"A goal without a plan is just a wish."*
>
> ~ Antoine de Saint-Exupéry

CHAPTER 13 - STEPPING STONES TO YOUR BEST LIFE

"I alone cannot change the world, but I can cast a stone across the waters to create many ripples." - Mother Teresa

As we sailed south, we encountered one of the coldest autumns the US eastern seaboard had ever experienced. Each day, we would rise from under countless blankets, start the coffee at stupid o'clock, and begin to assemble the many layers of clothing that we wore to keep ourselves warm. But then, suddenly, one day, we turned a corner. We were in Florida, headed to Daytona Beach. Until then, I had not managed to dress down to any less than three layers of clothing, but on that day, I was sailing in a t-shirt by midafternoon! I was convinced things were turning around.

While I firmly believe we cast our own shadow in this world, meaning that we choose our destiny, I also believe that the person we choose to become determines the energy that we emit to the universe, as well as the energy that surrounds us.

If you choose to live in negativity, you will be surrounded by a negative energy that will compound, and eventually swallow you, making it nearly impossible to break out of.

Similarly, how you treat others has an impact on the energy that surrounds you. I can attest personally that I have had moments in my life that I'm not proud of. I've allowed my emotions to get the best of me and treated others in an undesirable fashion. It typically leaves me in a foul mood, unable to concentrate, and generally unproductive.

Sadly, some people see fit to treat others as second-class just because they can. Somehow, they feel entitled to act in a way that defies the general rules of society and refuse to believe that a little thing called karma will ever come calling on them.

When we went sailing, we encountered someone like that. It was the day we moved onward from Daytona Beach, or more importantly, the day the weather started to consistently cooperate with us.

We were traveling down a marked, narrow channel of a much wider river. A power cruiser approached to pass us, well outside the channel markers. The vessel *Stardust* passed us at cruising speed, casting a dangerous 4' wake towards us that shook our boat violently from side to side. I braced myself against the helm as I watched items below deck flying about the cabin. Our two Alaskan Malamutes were on the fore deck, and luckily they knew to lie down, but it terrified them.

I radioed to *Stardust* and informed the captain of what I thought of his lack of respect in not slowing down to pass his fellow boaters. I received only a sarcastic reply.

Next, I radioed the six boats ahead which were travelling with us, warning them to be prepared for this inconsideration. Then I radioed the Coast Guard and alerted them that *Stardust* was just passing under the Mason Avenue Bridge, a federally regulated no-wake zone. I also notified them that he was throwing a 4-6' wake. The Coastguard took me to another channel, and gathered the details, thanked me, and bid me a nice day.

After we set anchor that evening, I received an emailed picture of *Stardust*, which was stuck aground. Later, when we met up with some of our buddy boats, *Tara*, from one boat, advised that as *Stardust* passed them, she saw a young woman and much older "gentleman" both wearing captain's hats. ONLY captain's hats.

Then, another buddy boater advised that the Coast Guard boarded *Stardust* and spent an hour inspecting his safety gear. They gave him a $135 fine for an expired fire extinguisher, then left. As they pulled away, *Stardust* radioed to them to report he was stuck aground. He insisted the Coast Guard needed to pull him off. The Coast Guard refused to assist, as they determined that *Stardust* was not in imminent danger, advising that high tide would dislodge him - in 12 hours.

When I heard this, I hoped that *Stardust* had learned an important lesson about how we treat others has a way of influencing how the universe treats us.

The following day, *Stardust* passed us again. This time in a much narrower channel. He radioed ahead, requesting a slow pass, and calmly drifted by us with no wake. He and his "mate" both had white uniforms on, as they smiled politely.

As you seek out your dream life, think about your actions, and how they will affect others. Take the time to reflect on your past when things didn't go as you hoped. Ask yourself what things you could have done differently, to cause a more positive outcome, not only for yourself, but for all those in your universe. Don't dwell on the less preferred outcome. Simply acknowledge that life presents us with options for change, but it's our job to recognize them, and determine how to utilize them. If you want to change your circumstances in life, often it requires that you change things about yourself first. It's nearly impossible to live the dream life, if you don't give proper attention to first becoming the person you want to be.

Whatever it is that you've defined as your dream life, remember that your legacy is what survives long after you're gone. A significant element of what defines your legacy are the principles you use to guide you. For me, some principles I learned of were easy to adopt, while others were more challenging. As we begin our careers we often think success is the most important principle, and that all other things must not impede that. Over time we can only hope we see that success on its own can be hollow, and meaningless. Its like winning a championship by not playing by the rules. A strong set of principles are those rules. Think of them not as rules governed by others, but rather rules you must govern yourself with.

Here are the key guiding principles that helped lead me to my dream life:

Eight Rules For A Better Life

Don't Take Yourself Too Seriously – As I've said many times already, as a youngster, I envisioned living a simple life. I imagined I would forever be fun loving and easy going. All characteristics that I never really noticed in my father. As I've mentioned, he was a serious man, and he didn't exactly buy into romance. At least not my vision.

Sadly, as the years morphed me from boy to man, I got more and more serious, to the point that I almost think I forgot how to smile. By the time I realized I was stuck, I had become a crusty nayhole younger Shawn would never have approved of.

I've since learned to loosen up, but I'm still a work in progress.

Be Careful to Whom You Share Your Ideas - As you navigate your way, you will inevitably come across people who will have opinions that differ from yours. Don't get me wrong, differing opinions can be a good thing. The caution I give you is about whom you chose to trust. Be sure that when you build your community, know who you can trust to give you sound advice. Be wary of people who will colour their advice with their bias.

Unfortunately, not all people have the capability to understand your vision, and some can even be governed by ulterior motives such as jealousy, or selfishness. So be aware that their advice could be tainted. That said, also be careful that you don't dismiss all advice that doesn't agree with your point of view, simply because it doesn't agree with your point of view.

Though my father and I saw the world differently in many ways, he was an excellent sounding board. He always wanted nothing but the best for me, and I knew that. By the time I was an adult, we both understood that we grew up in different times, which explained a lot about our different perspectives. So when I sought advice from him, it was offered and received with a mutual understanding of our differing points of view.

Have A Ride or Die - When you think of any historic accomplishment in our history, it's hard not to think of one that doesn't include a "right-hand person" or sidekick. Typically, the sidekick is much lesser known, if known at all, but still plays a critical role.

As you establish your plan for success, consider who can act as your sidekick, right-hand person, or ride or die. This should be a person who embraces your vision and wishes you nothing but unwavering success. Rely on this person as a valuable resource to bounce ideas off and bring a second set of eyes to the details of your plan.

Give More Than You Take - Throughout your journey, be mindful of the reputation you build for yourself. Are you a taker or a giver? We live in a world of finite resources at both a macro and micro level. If we all continuously take without giving back, it stands to reason that the time will come when there will be nothing left.

On an everyday level, this can be best understood by looking at your personal accountability. To the person who walks into a store and takes something without paying for it - do they understand that eventually the shopkeeper has to raise prices, go without, or possibly even go out of business if this continues? Likewise, when a person refuses to pay their contractor, or landscaper, or any number of services, someone else ends up going without.

At a different level, perhaps you're having a bad day. When you lean on others to get you through, pay them back if/when the storm is over, and better circumstances allow. Doing so will not only enhance your reputation, but it could also enable that person to change the lives of others.

Don't Strive to Be the Smartest, or Most Interesting Person - I spent much of my life thinking I was smart, and I worked hard to make others believe it as well. Even to this day, I occasionally get caught in the trap of believing that I'm interesting.

What I've come to discover, though is that life is much more rewarding when you take the time to discover how interesting other people are. As I reflect back, I realize that I've yet to meet a single person in my life who isn't smarter or better than me in some form or pursuit. Recognising this not only humbles you, but it also opens you up to a world of discovery and opportunity.

See Without Bias - Malcom Forbes *said "If you want understanding, try giving some";* I lived a great deal of my life without ever trying to understand the points of view of those whom I disagreed with. The most common result was that I would fail to get the result I desired. Once I resolved to open my eyes and try to appreciate the points of view of others, free of my own personal bias, I got much better at finding the common ground that paves the way for compromise, and win-win solutions.

Say It While You Can - Put simply, we are all just tourists on this place we call earth. None of us are permanent citizens, and none of us will get out alive.

While you can, take the time to say thank you. Remember to acknowledge those in your community for the good they bring to your life. Tell them what they mean to you and how much you would miss them if they were gone. It could keep them in your community for longer than otherwise might be the case.

Live Up to Your Expectations - As a former hockey coach, the one thing I could always count on, every season, was the mom or dad trying to live vicariously through their young superstar.

I remember one kid in particular who struggled all season to satisfy the expectations of both mom and dad. The last game of the season, I challenged him to go out and play just for himself. I asked him to believe in his own ability and play as well as he felt he could. I encouraged him to do it not for Mom or Dad, but just for himself. It was the best game he played all season!

When we set out to meet someone else's expectations, we waste time and energy worrying whether we measure up to their judgement. If and when we get feedback, its hard for us to accept it as honest if it's positive, and we become defensive if it's constructive.

More importantly, the expectation of others isn't necessarily reflective of what we want for ourselves. Your greatest energy always comes in moments when you are pursuing what's most important to you. As you plan and pursue your dream life, be sure its YOUR dream life!

Compass Point Reflections:

1) Leave A Good Footprint

Living your best life, your dream life, will require many things. Most of all it will require you to work hard everyday at being the person you want to be. If you are successful at that you will always be satisfied with the footprint you leave behind.

2) Be Your Own Judge

As you work to become the person you've always wanted to be don't let others decide how good of a job you're doing. You are the expert in that subject matter.

"Life shrinks or expands in proportion to one's courage." ~ Anais Nin

CHAPTER 14 – BUILDING YOUR COMMUNITY

"Talent wins games, but teamwork and intelligence win championships." ~ Michael Jordan

Greatness is not an individual sport. Have you ever watched anyone accept an award, and say, "Thank you, I did this completely on my own"? If you did, it's my guess that person alienated a lot of people around him/her.

The fact is, to achieve greatness is rarely a solo effort. There is almost always some type of community involvement. We sailed south as part of the *SAIL Magazine* "Sail to the Sun Rally" with 18 other boats. Each boat brought some skill or expertise to the effort. More than that, we had numerous people help us before we even got to the dock.

In Roatan, we utilized a total of 23 different contractors and sourced products from five different stores regularly. As challenging as it was at times, I learned to communicate in "Spanglish" to at least a near amateur level and made many friends who became part of my community.

To achieve your fullest potential, you will need to build a strong team and know how to treat them right. No matter whether you have a team of two or a team of many, the strength of your team depends on their ability, and willingness to commit to supporting you and your vision.

The Power of a Smile

Imagine you're walking down the street, so late for work you don't even have time to stop for your morning coffee.

Your alarm didn't go off because the power went out, thereby not charging your cell phone. You didn't even get a chance to shower before rushing out the door. Just when you think all hope is lost for the day, a friendly street vendor smiles at you as you walk past.

I've had days where I've been so raw that my first instinct was to snap, "What are you smiling at?" but then the power of that smile sinks in. Suddenly, you pause to realize that life simply isn't that bad.

When we see a smile, it serves as a reminder that we're on the right side of the grass and that life could be worse.

As I said in a previous chapter, I allowed myself to get so serious about life I think I forgot how to smile. For me, it got so bad that when I did smile, people often asked what I was up to. In fact, I think that the only time a smile came naturally to me was when I was on vacation.

Life should never be that way. A good smile is a kind of currency. When you walk into a store or business meeting, your smile sets the tone for the encounter. Even in the toughest negotiations, one should always strive for a win-win solution. A smile to start can serve as a reminder that nothing is personal and acknowledges the goal of the win-win outcome.

When you get up in the morning and look in the mirror, be sure to smile at the person looking back. I am certain you will appreciate and admire the smile you get back.

The Power of a Name

I started out my career openly acknowledging that I sucked at remembering names. I would go into a meeting with customers so focused on achieving my objectives I made no effort to remember names when I was introduced. What I failed to realize was just how important a name actually is to the person who owns it.

Studies show that one of the first terms that babies learn to recognize is their own name. One's name can carry a deep connection to who they are, and where they're from. It can also be an indicator of the culture they originate from. Learning and remembering a name, as well as proper pronunciation is a show of respect that can make a significant difference in the strength of the relationship you build.

When you meet someone new, be sure you hear the name clearly, without any misunderstanding. If it is a less common name, don't be afraid to ask how it is spelled, and spell it back, either in your head or aloud to them. If comfortable to do so, ask if the name has a certain meaning in a different language. If it's a common name, associate them with someone you know well who shares the same name. As much as is appropriate, use their name in a sentence to better engrave their name in your memory. If you are meeting with multiple people, and business cards are exchanged, try to lay the cards in positions reflective of where they are sitting.

Learning the power of recalling names will serve you well in life and help to gain the respect necessary to build a strong community.

Show Interest/Be Curious

Yes we did talk about this in previous chapters, but let's drill into it a bit deeper. If you desire to win anyone to your team or your way of thinking, you must take an interest in them. By this, I don't mean taking an interest in having them on your team. Your interest must be much deeper - it must be genuine. Get to know their hobbies, interests, and what family they have. In getting to know these things, you are learning about their favorite person - themselves.

This is a lesson I learned from my son, Daeyten. I mentioned that we were sailing south in the *SAIL Magazine* rally with a group of 18 boats. The average age of the crew was about 55-60. In spite of the significant age difference between Daeyten and the other crew members, he was by far the most popular "man on campus".

When we RV'd through Mexico, and when we set up in Roatan, it was the same. People much more advanced in age than him all loved him. He could change the mood of a room just by walking in.

What I discovered is that Daeyten took the time to get to know his community. He engaged in real conversations and took genuine interest. That resonated with them!

Acknowledgement

Have you ever had the pleasure of being acknowledged for a job well done? I remember times when I've walked the floor of manufacturing facilities with key leaders of the organization. A leader who is respected doesn't need any introduction. Workers instantly know who the person is. I've seen faces light up as bright as the sun when such a person stops to shake a hand and say thank you.

This reaction isn't something that's exclusive only to Presidents, CEO's, or famous people. Remembering to acknowledge someone in your life can also go a long way. Try walking into a coffee shop, addressing the barista by name, and smiling, before acknowledging her for the great coffee she made yesterday. It's almost certain that her day will improve from there. Equally important is that I bet she will try even harder to make you a great coffee tomorrow.

To get this right, you need only to be sincere, not over the top. Be sure that your acknowledgement passes the salt test and is a legitimate comment on a skill or a trait you know that person to possess. Sometimes, it can be exaggerated slightly if your goal is to lead them to put a greater expectation on themselves going forward.

By acknowledging a behavior you would like to see continue, you have rewarded that person's favorite person, themselves, and served notice that future good behavior will be noticed.

Compass Point Reflections:

1) Build a Stronger Community

In learning the techniques in this chapter you will undoubtedly strengthen your community. Be intentional about practicing them as much as possible. Eventually they will become habits that come naturally.

2) Solidify Your Place and Take Notes

As you practice these techniques and they eventually become natural to you it will solidify and likely even elevate your stature in your community. Be sure to journal about any differences you notice that come as a result.

"The most important single ingredient in the formula of success is knowing how to get along with people." ~
Theodore Roosevelt

CHAPTER 15 - THE POWER OF YOUR FIRST STEP

"Faith is taking the first step even when you don't see the whole staircase." ~ Martin Luther King, Jr.

By now you might be asking "Shawn, what exactly is YOUR dream life?". We started out thinking it was going sailing. Then we hopped in a motorhome and drove through Mexico. Then we bought the property in Roatan and opened the Jungle Reef Inn.

The one constant was freedom. We enjoyed the freedom to experience life as we dreamed it up. We aspired to see other parts of the world, and we set out to find them. Our sailing journey showed us an America we hadn't seen before. Then we headed to Mexico, and saw another country, and learned about another culture. We were warned many times that Mexico was scary and dangerous. We looked past that quasi reality and met Mexicans who were kind and generous to a fault.

In Roatan, we hosted people from 38 different countries. We brought the world to us. Again, we learned about different cultures, and soaked it all in. When I leave this world, I want to do so only after gaining a thorough understanding of the world and the many cultures that exist in it. That, I believe is my purpose.

I'll say it again that the difference between having a plan and executing a plan starts by taking the first step. No matter what vision you've created for yourself, nothing changes until you take that step.

The vision we create for a dream life can seem like it's a million miles away, and virtually impossible to realize. However, when you take the first step, you set in motion your plan, which can then lead to a second step, and third, and so on. Before you know it, you have momentum.

You probably know the word well, but for emphasis, *momentum* is defined in the Merriam-Webster dictionary as *"strength or force gained by motion or by a series of events"*.

It seems incredibly obvious that once you create a vision, detail a plan, and set your goals, taking the first step would be easy. While I sincerely wish that for you, its often anything but easy. Fear, conditioned belief, learned helplessness will all be things working against you. This is why it's important to be intentional and disciplined about taking that first step. What that first step is can be anything from major to minor – from stepping off a cliff to just stepping off a curb. Just be sure to be accountable about when and how you will take it. This reminds me of the saying "the way to move a mountain is one shovel load at a time". When you move that first shovel load, the job will seem overwhelming. If you keep your head down, staying focussed on the task, eventually the task will seem less overwhelming. Then you'll notice progress, until you eventually conclude the task is almost done, then done!

Psychological Momentum

To reinforce this point at a scientific level, I came across a study on something called *psychological momentum* In layman's terms, the theory is that as we accomplish tasks, we develop a tenacity or nothing-can-stop-me-now complex. As the result of several studies on this topic, many experts agree that psychological momentum is a force that is most effective when you approach a task with confidence, competence, and skill and start to achieve success. In your everyday life, I'm sure you've already experienced this as you went about routine daily chores. No sooner did you finish cleaning the bathroom then you said you could clean the whole house before it's time to pick up the kids. Most likely you exclaimed "I'm on a roll now!".

In major North American professional sports, it's consistent across baseball, basketball, and hockey that the team that wins the 1st game of a playoff series goes on to win the entire series approximately 65% of the time. While there are other factors that speak to this, the momentum gained from that first success is certainly a significant part of it.

> *"People give up because they don't know how close they are to success."* ~ Thomas Edison

If At First You Don't Succeed…

Something that may shock you is that success doesn't always happen on the first attempt. J.K. Rowland is now well known as the author of *Harry Potter* novels. Before she achieved that breakthrough success, she was severely depressed and nearly penniless. It took her 12 rejections before she finally found a publisher who believed in her work.

In 1976, two college dropouts founded a computer company. They set out to revolutionize the way computing was done and thought they could do so with a unique new approach. One of those two was named Steve Jobs, and the company was called, you guessed it, Apple Computers. While the technology they introduced was revolutionary, in 1985, Jobs was fired by Apple's board of directors. He went on to found another new company, NeXT Software and also bought Pixar, a huge success story all its own.

In 1997, while Apple was floundering, and at risk of failure, they bought out NeXT Software, asking Jobs to take on the role of CEO. By 2007 Apple launched the iPhone, one of the world's most successful products.

Dubbed by many as the greatest basketball player of all time, Michael Jordan was cut from his high school basketball team. Moreover, in his own words, he's admitted to having missed over 9000 shots in his career, lost almost 300 games, and on 26 occasions had been entrusted to take the game-winning shot and missed. He attributes his success to his failures.

The WWIP Method

So, what does it take to find success from failure? It's a little secret I like to call the WWIP Method. WWIP is an acronym for What, Why, Improve, Persevere. This formula is the difference between those who give up or continue to fail and those who find success from their failures.

When you don't achieve the result that you expect, the first thing you must ask yourself is *what did not work?*

In the case of Michael Jordon, he might have asked himself was it his shooting, his passing, his team play? What were the things that were not good enough to enable him to make the team?

At the end of each day on our boat, as we travelled south, we made a point to discuss what happened throughout the day. When something didn't happen as expected or planned, we discussed why it didn't happen as planned. Then we developed strategies to achieve success next time around.

Once you determine what didn't work, the next thing you need to do is to understand why. If I failed to close a sale, one of the surest ways to gain knowledge of why is to ask. I would solicit feedback directly from the customer. Who is more qualified to tell you why they don't see things your way than the very person who doesn't see things your way.

Sadly, one of the most common mistakes salespeople make is the inability or unwillingness to ask why. As I've stated previously, we're all in sales in one way or another. If you come up short of the result you desire, determine why.

Once you know the what and the why, you now have the tools to go back and improve. This reminds me of the saying, "The definition of insanity is doing the same thing over and over and expecting a different result." ~ Albert Einstein.

The fact is, as many as 80% of people get tripped up in this step. These are the people who either 1) give up too soon 2) repeat the same process, hoping for a different result, or 3) start over from scratch.

Instead of throwing the baby out with the bath water, so to speak, determine the what, the why, and use this information to determine how to improve your process to address what didn't work in your previous attempt.

Most importantly, persevere. The world is full of examples of failure before success. The Wright Brothers failed before they succeeded with their first flight. Henry Ford had two failed automobile companies, before he succeeded in producing the first production automobile. Thomas Edison tested thousands of materials before creating the carbon-filament lightbulb.

Where would the world be if any of these people had given up after the first attempt?

As the date to vacate our last property, September 30, grew closer, I would be lying if I said it didn't cause stress. I was happy with the decision we had made and looking forward to the adventure that awaited. Yet, I still struggled to silence the Headshaker, as it seemed determined to convince me I was making the biggest mistake in my life.

I would wake up in the middle of the night in a cold sweat, asking myself what I was doing. I was giving up the safe life that I resented but had become so accustomed to.

While psychological momentum continued to push me forward, knowing my WHAT helped me to erase many doubts. By reminding myself that my life had become little more than an existence and comparing it to the balance that I was certain was waiting for me in my journey, I gained the courage to silence the Headshaker. The adage "That which doesn't kill you makes you stronger" seemed so relevant to me then. As long as our adventure didn't kill us, I had zero doubt that I would be stronger for it, no matter how it turned out. That was my WHAT will change.

You will need to define the steps that will move you towards your own point of no return. Be sure to acknowledge the successes that will help you build your psychological momentum and be prepared to temper the big steps with smaller ones.

Know that you will face moments of adversity, which you will inevitably overcome. Remind yourself often of what will change for you when you realize the vision that you've planned so carefully for.

Compass Point Reflections:

1) Ride the Momentum

Once you begin to achieve success, don't let the momentum be lost. Recognize it and use it to your advantage.

2) The WWIP Method

When setbacks occur, determine WHAT went wrong, WHY it went wrong, IMPROVE your process, and PERSEVERE.

3) What will change?

Never lose sight of why you are working so hard to affect change.

"Shoot for the moon. Even if you miss, you'll land among the stars." ~ Norman Vincent Peale

CHAPTER 16: TAME THE STRESS MONSTER

"Just because you take breaks doesn't mean you're broken." ~ Curtis Tyrone Jones

Burnout is Real… and Dangerous

Before I made the decision to go sailing, I wore burnout like a badge of honor. I was travelling extensively and found it almost impossible to shut down at the end of the day. I absorbed myself in my work and would reply to emails at all hours of the day or night. I had grown my division from start-up to $7M per year in three years. I had edged out my peers, to win the Chairman's Club Award of Sales Excellence three years consecutively and was poised to explode that growth into the US market. I had become addicted to success and the recognition that came with it. In my mind, I felt that burnout was something that wasn't a danger. I was handling it, and I would be fine.

Then, the new VP came along, and suddenly things were different. Until then I was surrounded by people who appreciated the results being generated by my team. Now, they seemed to not matter. Suddenly, I wasn't as motivated to get up in the morning. The nights alone in a hotel room got emptier. That badge of honor now looked tarnished and ugly. It made me question what I was doing this for and at what cost.

Success at whatever you choose to pursue can become addictive. For many, the more success you achieve, the more you crave it. Experts say this is because your brain produces a chemical called dopamine. I'll ask you to consult with the experts if you want to fully understand the scientific effects and explanation, but to summarize in the best layman's terms I can cobble, dopamine is produced in the brain when we win, and it is addictive.

So, as you find success in your journey, be aware. I was not the first nor the last career-driven warrior to wear stress like a badge of honor while on a path to conquer the corporate world, working 6-7 days a week and seldom shutting down. That was me for a significant part of my life. I would travel all week, working in the hotel room after a long day. When I arrived home after a long travel day, I would kiss my wife and kids, then sit on the couch, and check emails. Saturday morning, more emails, while I created a list of follow ups from the week that passed. The business made me feel needed and important. As I was busy making myself larger than life in my own mind, my community, and in particular my family, were drifting away from me. Worse than that, my healthy self was quickly dying. I was burning out, while thinking that made me a hero. It didn't.

I knew I needed to change that day on the plane. As I looked out the window, it occurred to me that heroes are people who treasure the things they love most and are willing to sacrifice for them. My sacrifices were being made for money and recognition. Those weren't things I loved. Staring out that plane window, I realized that I was making sacrifice for a man who would, and did, throw me under the bus just to make himself look better. I also realized that my family and my Self pillars were the ones being sacrificed.

I loved my job. I educated people on how to build warmer, more energy-efficient homes. I travelled all around North America and got to meet many interesting people. It was challenging and rewarding. But my job, on its own, wasn't enough. As I obsessed with making another sale, and in my imperious mind, getting one step closer to saving the world, I recognized that it was time to save myself. I was burned out. Admitting it didn't mean I was weak or any less capable of doing my job. In fact, it meant that if I was going to keep doing my job as well as I was, I needed to develop some strategies to balance my life and save myself.

Regardless of where you are in your career, you should be aware of the symptoms and effects of burnout syndrome.

Here is a symptoms questionnaire taken directly from the Mayo Clinic website:

Job burnout symptoms:

To find out if you might have job burnout, answer these questions:

- *Do you question the value of your work?*
- *Do you drag yourself to work and have trouble getting started?*
- *Do you feel removed from your work and the people you work with?*
- *Have you lost patience with co-workers, customers, or clients?*
- *Do you lack the energy to do your job well?*
- *Is it hard to focus on your job?*
- *Do you feel little satisfaction from what you get done?*
- *Do you feel let down by your job?*
- *Do you doubt your skills and abilities?*

- *Are you using food, drugs, or alcohol to feel better or to numb how you feel?*
- *Have your sleep habits changed?*
- *Do you have headaches, stomach or bowel problems, or other physical complaints with no known cause?*

If you answered yes to any of these questions, you might have job burnout. Think about talking to a healthcare professional or a mental health professional. These symptoms also can be linked to health conditions, such as depression.

Taken from that same page, here are some of the common risk factors that contribute to burnout, as well as the associated costs of burnout:

Job burnout risk factors

The following factors can add to job burnout:

- *Having a heavy workload and working long hours.*
- *Struggling with work-life balance.*
- *Working in a helping profession, such as health care, that involves a lot of giving to others.*

- *Feeling of having little or no control over work.*

Costs of job burnout

Doing nothing about job burnout can make the problems worse. As a result, you might:

- *Feel drained.*
- *Feel unable to cope.*
- *Not be able to sleep.*
- *Be sad, angry, irritable or not care.*
- *Use more alcohol or other substances.*
- *Get heart disease, high blood pressure or type 2 diabetes.*
- *Be more likely to get sick.*

The Three Pillars Guide to a Balanced Life

In chapter 2, I introduced the principles of the Three Pillars of a Balanced Life and talked about how achieving a healthy self is the foundation that supports a healthy Community/Family Pillar, as well as a healthy Career Pillar. Let's expand on some strategies that will help you to build a strong Self Pillar foundation:

Good Time Management - Work schedules can be rigid and demanding, but don't allow them to monopolize you. Build a schedule that takes your responsibilities into account but be sure to include time for your Self and community pillars. Literally schedule into your calendar times when you will be unplugged, be it for family time, meditation, exercise, and the other items you need to achieve balance. Start out by being ridged with this schedule, recognizing that commitment to Self pilar time and community pillar time is just as important as Career time.

Over time, you will become aware of how productive unplugged time can be. When you reach that point, you can start to be more flexible in bartering Self time for Community or Career time as situations demand. Starting with a ridged routine, is key to developing a strong, balanced commitment to all three pillars.

Control the Narrative - As situations occur in your life, take time to think about them. At the end of the day, or the beginning of the next, consider the obstacles or challenges you faced. Consider what went well, and what didn't go quite as planned.

Think about these things in context of what you did to create that success and what you could have done differently to avoid setbacks. This is a process of learning that there are two types of outcomes: a preferred outcome and an opportunity to learn. Either way, appreciate that while you don't control all circumstances, you do control how you react to all circumstances.

Our natural tendency is to dwell on the negative when we don't get the result we need or expect. Our energy is much better spent being focused on what progress was made, and what changes are required for further advance progress.

Mindfulness Meditation - The principles of mindfulness meditation are simple. It is a practice of bringing your awareness to the here and now. Our minds often tend to wander ahead of the current situation. I found myself doing this frequently when we went sailing. At night, I would think about the next day's sail. At rest, my undisciplined mind would imagine what could go wrong. I would think about mechanical failures, or bad weather, or any number of worst-case scenarios.

Using the practice of mindfulness meditation, I would go to a quiet place, bring my mind back to present reality and focus on the true characteristics of the current moment. I would think about where I was, and what was happening in that exact place and time. I would rule out the option to imagine any false realities.

I strongly encourage you to do your own research on mindfulness meditation and include it in your routine.

Exercise, Stretching, and Yoga - The benefits of exercise are many. Daily exercise can greatly improve your overall health and wellbeing. For physical health, it can increase your cardiovascular endurance, strength, and flexibility. This will help to reduce your risk of developing chronic diseases such as heart disease, diabetes, and obesity.

Daily exercise can also help to improve your mental health by reducing stress and anxiety levels and improving your mood and self-esteem.

Exercise releases endorphins, which are natural mood-boosters that can help to alleviate feelings of depression and anxiety.

In addition, having a daily exercise routine can improve your cognitive function and memory, as well as your sleep quality.

Exercise helps to promote the growth of new brain cells and improve neural connections, which can lead to improved cognitive function and memory.

Don't forget that as we age, our body has a natural tendency to tighten up. So, including a regular stretching routine in your daily practice is a phenomenal way to re-energize, and prepare for the rigors of your day.

Remember that yoga is a great way to combine stretching and exercise into one practice.

Together, these benefits give you an indisputable advantage in building a heathy, balanced life.

Controlled Breathing - Controlled breathing is a great tool that helps manage stress and regain focus.

What is controlled breathing? It is a technique that involves consciously regulating the pace and depth of your breaths. It allows you to control your body's stress response and promote relaxation. By focusing on your breath, you can increase oxygen intake, slow your heart rate, and calm your mind.

Controlled breathing activates the relaxation response, easing tension and reducing stress hormones.

By bringing oxygen to the brain, controlled breathing enhances focus, concentration, and cognitive performance. Controlled breathing supports a healthy immune system, lowers blood pressure, and boosts overall wellness.

Before important meetings, as well as any event that could elevate my stress levels, I make it regular practice to set a few moments aside, in order to use this practice.

Here are three common techniques:

1) Box Breathing

A powerful technique that involves inhaling, holding, exhaling, and holding again in equal counts, creating a calming rhythm.

2) Deep Belly Breathing

Focusing on slow, deep breaths that expand and contract the diaphragm, promoting relaxation and reducing anxiety.

3) 4-7-8 Breathing

Breathe in for a count of 4, hold for a count of 7, and exhale for a count of 8. This pattern helps to regulate the breath and induce calmness.

Be sure to find a quiet space, sit comfortably with your spine straight, close your eyes and bring your focus to your breath.

Controlled breathing is not only effective for stress reduction or before an important presentation to calm nerves. It can also be practiced before sleep to induce relaxation for better sleep quality or during challenging situations to manage emotions effectively.

Anytime you need a moment of tranquillity in a busy day, incorporate controlled breathing into various aspects of your life and reap the rewards.

Numerous studies have been done that have concluded that controlled breathing is a powerful tool for reducing stress and enhancing well-being, improving cognitive function, while achieving a calmer state of mind.

Enjoy Nature - While I am not a licensed therapist, and certainly don't recommend nature as an alternative to professional therapeutic services for those who need it, it has been said many times, by many people, that nature is a great form of therapy. Whether you choose to hike deep into the woods, or sit by the sea, going outdoors is a great way to clear your head, and collect your thoughts.

Eating Healthy - An all too easily forgotten tool is healthy eating. I know this better than many, having practically lived in hotels and restaurants for much of my career. I'm sure many of you can identify with the unhealthy routine that business travel fosters.

You're up early to prepare for the meetings the day has to offer, and struggle to get a healthy breakfast. Lunch and dinner are much the same, often followed by drinks with customers, and/or co-workers.

For me, this routine led to high blood pressure and too many extra pounds. It had negative effects on my sleeping habits, confidence, and caused increased stress, and moodiness. Establishing healthy, balanced eating habits has benefited my overall well-being in so many ways, I believe it saved my life.

Good Night's Sleep and the Power Nap - Most of us know that a good night's sleep is a valuable tool for getting a good start to the day. Studies show that the amount of sleep you get is less important than the quality of sleep. So always try to check your thoughts at the bedroom door. Whatever didn't get done today will be there for you to do tomorrow, but getting a good night's sleep will see you approaching that task with a clearer mind, generally ensuring more positive outcomes. Don't overlook the power of a 10-minute power nap in the middle of the day. For some, 10 minutes of exercise works best for clearing the mind, while many argue that the power nap makes them a new person. Whatever works best for you, take it guilt-free, knowing that it will make you more productive, innovative, and a better problem solver.

Reading and Journalling - While we've touched on journalling several times, I'll say it once more. As we go through life, we face many challenges. Sometimes you experience adversity that seems overwhelming in a moment, but when you look back at it later, you see it as almost inconsequential. Other experiences you reflect back on can remind you of solutions that you've since forgotten about. What's almost undeniable is that journalling is an excellent tool for helping us measure and acknowledge our growth. It is also a great way for us to learn from ourselves, just as reading is great a way to learn from others. Make it a regular practice to set aside a part of each day to do both.

Social Support - Worded differently, social support is described as your community/family pillar. I've talked about how a strong, healthy Self pillar is the foundation of a healthy community/family, and career pillar. What we must not overlook is how interwoven social support is, for building a healthy self.

No matter what your mission in life is, you will encounter adversity. No matter how well you prepare for your journey, the day will likely come when you're at the brink of collapse, out of energy, and questioning whether you can go on.

If/when that day comes, it will be your social network who will come to your aid, lifting you up and inspiring you to persevere.

In my life, my network is small, but I know there are people I can count on. I'm keenly aware of their strengths which enables me to know who to call on for which need. Get to know your network and get to know how you can serve them. In doing so, it will afford you an opportunity to understand who will be there for you when you need them.

Compass Point Reflections:

1) Take Your Well Being Seriously

Get informed, be proactive, and remember that courage is knowing when you've had enough.

2) Live by the Laws of the Three Pillars

Your Self pillar is your foundation - don't allow it to crack. The other two pillars are the walls - they need to support each other. Together, they build an indestructible pyramid when they're equally served.

3) Don't be afraid to talk.

If not for yourself, do it for those who love you.

"Live as if you were to die tomorrow. Learn as if you were to live forever." ~ Mahatma Gandhi

CHAPTER 17 - TIME TO NAVIGATE

"In the fields of observation, chance favors only the prepared mind." ~ Louis Pasteur

There's a saying, "You've got to be good to be lucky, and lucky to be good".

As your plan transforms into progress, beware of forces commonly referred to as synchronicity. Some believe in these forces unreservedly, while others will argue till the end of time that no such thing exists, and that we are 100% responsible for our own success in life. You might even be confused that I mention such a mystical thing.

"Hamill, you tell me to stop being a passenger and take control of my own life, and now you're telling me to believe in this magical force?" is what I imagine you thinking right now.

It's true, to get what you want from life, you MUST take the wheel, know your destination, and have a plan to get there. But I've also mentioned the *rumble strip effect* This is the bumpy edge found on some highways, designed to warn you that you're about to drive into a ditch. It warns me on occasion when I've driven while tired.

It's never efficient to drive the bus we call life over on the rumble strip. It will be a bumpy ride that will get you nowhere fast. Yet, we just might come to accept this path if we endure it for too long. Worst yet, some of us might lose hope and simply stop driving altogether.

After you've brought clarity to your vision and equipped your toolbox with the things you need to realize it, driving down the centre of your lane makes driving easier and results in a much smoother ride.

Once you get on that clear path, success still isn't guaranteed, but there is a school of thought that it opens up for broader, and more plentiful possibilities. The key is to have an open mind that will see those possibilities. Sometimes to discover success you must see those possibilities differently.

The scientific community attributes many important discoveries to synchronicity, a classic example being the discovery of X-rays. In 1895, German physicist Wilhelm Roentgen discovered x-rays while studying the effects of passing electric current through partially evacuated glass tubes. Put simply, he discovered X-rays simply by accident, but it was the result of an observant mind.

When I took that flight into Tampa Bay, the flight path did not include multiple passes over the Gulf of Mexico. We were delayed getting out of Toronto due to bad weather, and that delay meant we had to circle Tampa until they could clear a landing window for us. If my flight had been on time, who knows if an awakening would have presented itself to me. However, when that clarity did present itself it was fortunate that I had the open mind to receive the message.

If you resolve to drive through life on the rumble strip, you become so obsessed with the discomfort of the ride, you're likely to miss the signs for the offramps that will lead you to where you're supposed to be.

When you become intentional about taking control of your life and resolve to making a plan that gets you off the rumble strip, you set yourself up for the success that you desire and end the cycle of undermining yourself. Whether there are mystical forces that become our allies when we set ourselves up for success is a philosophy we can choose to believe in, or not. If you wish to gain a better understanding of this concept, I encourage you to do more research on "The flow state".

What we should all be able to agree on is that each of us are in control of our own path. When you accept that, your path can lead you to limitless opportunities you open up a world of possibilities that are limited only by your imagination.

Some call this Blue Sky thinking. When the Wright brothers imagined they could fly, they were guilty of Blue Sky thinking, both literally and figuratively.

Going back even further, Christopher Columbus envisioned that the world wasn't flat, but round, and that he could find a way to India that wasn't fraught with the perils of long land passages.

Again, this is an example of someone who did not think within the confines of what was known as fact, but rather opened his mind to explore possibility without limitations.

As you develop your vision, and proceed on your journey, embrace these principles of Blue Sky thinking.

The Domino Effect

When I was a young boy, I was fascinated with dominos. My grandfather and grandmother had many of them, as they were avid players of the strategic game of dominos.

For me, though, dominos had a much greater purpose. I would create a line of dominos standing on end in order. Once I set them all up, in line, I would tip the 1st one over and watch as it created a chain reaction. In order, each domino would proceed to knock over the next tile until no more were standing. What started as a small step of knocking over a single tile would become an almost unstoppable chain reaction. It's called the domino effect.

As you put your plan into motion and start building momentum the domino effect is likely to take hold. As you complete one step, then the next, and the next, be alert to the new opportunities that will be almost spontaneously generated from those previous steps. Be sure to maintain an open mind to see the opportunities unfold, but don't allow yourself to get overwhelmed. Just breathe.

Eyes On the Journey

When you reach this point, spiking the football in celebration isn't the only thing left to do. Life is about the journey, not the destination. In fact, it's my contention that the destination of life is a place we generally try to avoid for as long as we can. It's that moment when our life is about to end, as we gasp our last breaths. In most cases, we don't get much chance to effect change once we've reached the destination.

However, we should always be thinking about change during the journey. I'm reminded of a young lad of 14 years old whom I once coached in hockey. He was a goaltender, and he was good. I believed at the time that he could have played professional hockey if he kept working hard and finding ways to continue his development.

We were in the midst of playoffs, and he was playing well. When I asked him what he was going to work on in that practice he reiterated that he felt he was playing quite well and didn't have anything that he needed to improve.

Professional athletes get to the professional level because they chose to be exceptional. That takes continuous improvement, which is why they're usually the first to show up for practice and the last to leave. They know that others are always trying to reach their level of excellence, which makes them work even harder at getting better. That's what keeps them elite - that commitment to practice and continuous improvement. Elite performers, in any discipline, are always moving the goalposts on their goals and objectives.

Before you reach maximum velocity and the domino effect engages, I caution you to be prepared. Reaching this point is the overriding objective of your whole plan. You don't want to have to destroy that momentum because you didn't properly prepare for it. That would be comparable to the elite athlete getting his shot to play at the professional level, and then realize he didn't train hard enough in the off-season, and as a result, wasn't in the proper condition for training camp.

Once you reach maximum velocity, do not allow yourself to fall into the trap of thinking about destination. Recognize that you have simply reached another milestone of the journey and continue to develop the next steps. Always be sure to have additional stops planned beyond the leg you are working on. This will prevent you from losing momentum and ending up back at stuck.

When we were sailing, I believed maximum velocity to be around when we reached the southern part of Georgia. We had become accustomed to our new boat and finally got it running the way we wanted. It took us until then to finally get our chart plotter working properly, which was a significant factor in helping us to determine our bearings. We had also gotten into a good routine of what time to head out each morning and the regimen required to get on our way. By then, we knew exactly who would do what. We had a system that was defined and was working.

But this is the point where you can easily be lulled into a false sense of security. You bring yourself to think things are running so well that nothing can set you back. It is the opposite of the life on the rumble-strip mentality.

For us, we stopped looking ahead to consider the circumstance we needed to plan for. As we headed into Florida, we woke up one morning to an intense fog bank that completely disrupted our routine of a 6:30 am departure. What's worse is that once the fog finally did lift, we headed out without checking the weather ahead of us. While our original plan was to end the day in St. Augustine, we ended up in a race to Jacksonville with another storm, and major fog bank, closing in on us from the east. We managed to get to the dock just as the storm bared down on us, followed by a fog thick enough to cut with a chainsaw!

It was then that we started to realize we needed to expand the range of our planned journey. To that point, we had resolved to get to South Florida. Our method was simply getting up each morning, in time for a 6:30 am departure, and sailing for 6-8 hours, or whatever it took to find a safe anchorage.

We had gone into auto-pilot mode. It was threatening our potential for growth and purpose.

Trust Your Inner Compass

Through all of the previous chapters, we've discussed finding out who you are, who you are meant to become, and discovering what you truly want in life. The rest is merely a recipe to help get you there.

In Chapter Three, we talked about the six ingredients of fulfillment. If you follow this recipe, it will help you on the road. However, the road will present many twists, turns and forks along the way.

To successfully navigate, you must find your inner compass. Not only that, but you must also learn how to use your inner compass, including how to trust in your compass. Don't be surprised if there's a learning curve to using your inner compass. Unfortunately, it doesn't come with instructions. Take comfort in knowing that the path you choose rarely results in dead ends, and if it does, there is no shame in backtracking to an alternate course.

While the goal of the journey is to discover the six ingredients of fulfillment, the blessing of the journey is enlightenment. You will achieve a discovery of yourself, and the world around you, that will bring clarity, and comfort. But know that enlightenment is only achieved by the accepting mind that travels the journey with an openness and willingness to accept it.

The only real advice I can give you about learning to trust your inner compass is that the trust will strengthen as you progress, as long as you keep an open mind.

Compass Point Reflections:

1) Keep an open mind on your journey, watching for synchronicity along the way.
2) Embrace the Domino Effect
3) Trust Your Inner Compass

"Inner guidance is heard like soft music in the night by those who have learned to listen." ~ Vernon Howard

CHAPTER 18 - COLLATERAL BEAUTY

"I can't change the direction of the wind, but I can adjust my sails to always reach my destination."

~ Jimmy Dean

2016 saw the launch of a movie called Collateral Beauty starring Will Smith.

Smith plays lead character "Howard" who is a brilliant advertising executive, who loses his child to cancer. He allows this tragic circumstance to nearly destroy him, withdrawing from almost everything that shaped his life up to that point. Over the course of the movie, he challenges the universe for answers by writing letters to Love, Time, and Death. When those letters are answered unexpectedly, it begins to challenge his perspective. Eventually Howard comes to the realization that even in the event of a horrible tragedy, the collateral beauty of one's life should never be forgotten.

In more universal terms, we must make a point of ensuring that the beauty of any experience is never completely overshadowed by negative moments that occur as a part of that experience.

Not long after we settled into the marina in Key Largo we discovered a crack in our mast. We were about to head home for Christmas. We had just finished the Sail to the Sun Rally in Miami, Florida and said goodbye to the other 18 boats that we were travelling with. Our plan was to dock the boat at Marina Del Mar and drive 24 hours straight in a rental car to get home by Christmas Eve - unannounced.

Life was good until I discovered that 8" gash about a foot up from the deck. My initial reaction was devastation. We spent more than budgeted on the purchase of our boat. So we definitely did not have money in the budget for a $30,000 mast replacement. 24 hours of windshield time is a lot of time for a shift in perspective to occur.

My shift in perspective began when I acknowledged that we had just competed an extraordinary adventure that I had to be thankful for. The boat held up beautifully until then, and now our plan was to rest there until we were ready to move on. If this was destined to happen, it happened at the best time possible.

Coming to this realization enabled me to move beyond destroyed, envision the collateral beauty of the bigger picture and start thinking with clarity again. I started by reaching out to my network, and soon had an expert I could lean on for advice on how to have the mast repaired or replaced. Another contact suggested that I ask the insurance company if it was covered. Long story short, we developed a plan that averted disaster after I shifted my perspective.

Our default instinct is to focus on the worst part of a story and allow that to shape the narrative. When we zoom out, we often see the light instead of the darkness. It changes our entire experience and helps to lead us forward toward fulfilment.

If you have made it this far, I want to thank you for sticking with me. I hope that I have inspired you to not only dare to dream but also to spread your wings and fly. I'm far from a perfect man, but I'm working hard at living the perfect life for me. I suspect that if you took the time to read this far, then you and I are very much alike. Possibly, one thing that distinguishes us is that I dared to dream, and then I dared to pursue that dream - I challenge you to do the same!

As I mentioned previously, our journey had its ups and downs. There was the low of me making bad decisions on Chesapeake Bay, which lead to Daeyten wanting to quit on us. In contrast there was the Dismal Swamp, when most of our 18-boat fleet rafted together on a dock meant for 3 boats. Over two days we went from strangers, to friends, to a tight knit community with a common purpose.

There was the unseasonable cold front that enveloped the eastern seaboard for most of the journey, making for long, cold days of sailing. Then there was the warm receptions we received from town to town that melted our chills away.

We made it to Miami, FL, on December 21, 2014, and celebrated by spending the day on a little island, just across the channel from downtown, called Luijo's Island. Several of our buddy boats also anchored in the bay surrounded by Miami Marine Stadium. By midafternoon, we had our first group beach party happening on this small island, and we even broke out our swimsuits!

 As our buddy boaters joined us on the island, we toasted to three lightly experienced boaters on a new-to-them boat, overcoming their anxieties and completing the first leg of the journey. We joked that due to the unseasonable cold the trip was, at times, miserable. Then acknowledged it was a misery we would never have traded for anything.

The next day, we attended a reception sponsored by *Sail Magazine*, to mark the official end of the Sail to the Sun

Rally. Two days later, we headed out of Biscayne Bay onto the Atlantic, destined for Key Largo.

Upon arriving at Marina Del Mar we parked the boat, picked up a rental car, and prepared to head home for Christmas. Having just completed the trip of a lifetime, we planned to use the 24 hours of driving time to decompress and discuss what we just experienced.

It was while we were cleaning up the boat, and battening down the hatches, that we noticed the crack in the mast, which certainly added another dimension to the thoughts we had to process while driving.

As great as it was to live this experience, it was even greater to surprise our families, as we showed up, unannounced, on Christmas Eve, and told them of our journey.

December 31, 2014, we returned to our re-named boat, *Suenos (Spanish for Dreams)*, ready to continue the journey. We spent 2 ½ months in Florida before heading back north for my busy season with the business.

By the time the dust had settled on our sailing adventure, we sailed over 2500 nautical miles. We travelled through nine states, making it as far south as Key West, before arriving back in Canada on June 15, 2015 aboard *Suenos*.

The people who arrived back in Canada that day were not the same people who left aboard a 30' rented RV on September 30, 2014. The experience changed us forever.

Six years earlier, as Leanne and I were on our first date, I pledged to her that I was going to go sailing one day. Then suddenly, we were back in Canada having done it. Many thought we were crazy, just for dreaming such a dream. It didn't matter - we were chasing a dream. It was OUR dream, and the opinions of others were not going to kill it. Ironically, I believe it was my father who understood that the most!

Then came the RV trip through Mexico the following year, before "settling down" in the fall of 2016 in Roatan, Honduras.

For me, the greatest blessing I've been given is that I have learned to appreciate the collateral beauty of every experience this life offers. To the saying every cloud has a silver lining, I say the silver lining can only be seen by appreciative, willing eyes.

So, as you embark on your path become intentional about enjoying the experience. Don't allow yourself to become so focused on the destination that you forget to witness the beauty of the journey. You have but one life to live, so be intentional about enjoying that life. If you have ever whispered, "One day I will…" throw that term out, and replace it with "On this day I will…" and "Today I am…"

In doing this, commit to yourself that when the end comes, you will be full of memories, not regrets!

Compass Point Reflections:

1) This one is for YOU

    Write down 3 take aways that stand out as most important to you. They can be dreams, goals, lessons you've learned or just about anything, so long as they resonate as important to you. Then ask yourself "what are you going to do with this?".

"You miss 100% of the shots you don't take."

~ Wayne Gretzky

EPILOGUE

Closing the Loop

When we purchased our property in Roatan, it was to be our chance to settle down. I had pledged that I was going to live a simple life, but "live" was the optimal word. I no longer wanted to spend 70 nights per year in a hotel room alone. But we still needed to make a living. In my mind, I saw it as a sort of long-term commitment to the simple life Dreamer Shawn had envisioned so many years previous. While it wasn't selling t-shirts on the beach, it was selling hotel room nights near the beach… with a great view of the ocean.

The building that we purchased was an old wood building perched on the side of a steep hill, that was long overdue for an overhaul. It took some doing to bring her back to beauty, but we did it, fueled by the vision that Dreamer Shawn had created. It took about 9 weeks, and a lot of blood, sweat and tears, from a lot of people. But the process was invigorating.

What happened next was very unexpected. When the long days of renovations gave way to lazy days of watching bananas grow on our property, and lazing on the beach, I began to feel a sense of emptiness. We would wake up early, eager to be up to serve any needs our guests might have. Once they headed out for the day, we tackled a list of routine tasks that were typically complete by noon. The rest of the day was ours, to enjoy beach life. I wasn't even 50 yet, we were making a comfortable living, and our most time-consuming task was going to the beach. What was not to love?

Responsible Shawn had other thoughts. Ironically, Dreamer Shawn didn't necessarily disagree with him. For some people, the life I was living would have been all they would ever need. Sadly, I wasn't wired like that. I've articulated that in order to live a balanced live, we must serve all three pillars. I've also articulated that the Self pillar serves as the foundation that supports all three pillars. What I discovered is that in order to build a happy, healthy Self pillar, you must satisfy all three personas that make up our Self pillar. As we enjoyed our beach life, it seemed that none of the three personas were being properly served, including Dreamer Self.

Don't get me wrong… Dreamer Shawn likes simple and loves the beach and the ocean. But Dreamer Shawn found emptiness from knowing that my other two personas were not being satisfied. While Dreamer Shawn was getting a wholesome dose of simple beach life, Responsible Shawn still needed growth, accomplishment, and purpose. The lack thereof affected Dreamer Shawn, perhaps as much as it did Responsible Shawn. That emptiness awoke the Headshaker, who asserted the notion that I was wasting my life and my talents by rotting on the beach.

My discovery was that purpose, and fulfillment, does not come from excess but rather from balance. To realize fulfillment in your life, you must achieve balance. We've examined the three pillars of a balanced life, and the role they play.

The emptiness I still felt while living my simple life drove me to dig deeper. That is when I realized how important it is to have three healthy, happy self personas that not only co-exist but are equally served.

Naturally, you might be asking, "Why would you want to serve the disruptive Headshaker persona?" The truth is that ultimately our Headshaker persona is not a destructive force merely for the purpose of being a destructive force. The Headshaker within all of us is there to always be considering what could be wrong and what could go wrong. In having two well balanced, healthy personas being the Responsible Self and Dreamer self, the Headshaker is silenced and content to co-exist in harmony.

Once that is achieved, the Headshaker has little else to complain about other than maybe religion, and politics… and the fact the Toronto Maple Leafs still have not won a Stanley Cup in my lifetime as of this moment.

With this awareness, Leanne and I left Roatan in the spring of 2017, originally to care for my father in Canada who was suffering from the advanced stages of a rare form of cancer. We put a team of people in place on site to help run the local operations while overseeing everything remotely. This gave us a broader opportunity to keep the simple life alive while caring for my father and seeking out projects that served Responsible Shawn.

When my father passed away in August of 2017, he did so only after making it clear that he supported who I had become. He didn't always understand me but always supported me. Perhaps the two of us collectively are actually a part of something even bigger that I've yet to understand with him playing the role of Responsible and of course me playing Dreamer?

Once my father's affairs were settled and my mother had sorted out her where-to-go-from-here, we resolved to go back to Roatan to continue our beach life. Just before we made final arrangements, I was recruited by a building materials company with an opportunity to head back into a corporate role. I was hired as a National Accounts manager and asked to re-locate to Canada's west coast.

I took with me the insight I gained from the collective of my experiences of the past four years. I resolved that I would serve my three pillars equally with a focus on the needs of each of my three personas. While this new balance enhanced the wellbeing of my Self and Community pillars, it also enabled me to serve my Career pillar in a way I don't think existed previously. Now conceding that my Career pillar, on it's own, was not the most important component of my life, I gained confidence and security – it made me a better contributor in the corporate world. Where before I was much more reluctant to contribute to forces of change, I now recognized that my contributions were valuable even if not adopted. Suddenly, it was ok to be a disruptor.

The perspective I gained about what's important in life helped me to operate at a higher intensity rate while working, then switch gears smoothly to my other pillars without doubt or guilt. All around I was happier, healthier, and no longer feeling trapped. I had seen what lied beyond the corporate world. On it's own, it didn't have everything

I needed, but neither did corporate life. Now I knew how to find balance between the two worlds.

This is the point of enlightenment I hope for you. Committing to and adopting change in the pursuit of your dream life is the beginning. Incorporating the 6 Fundamentals of Fulfillment is a key part of the process. But to close the loop, one must learn the lessons that the journey teaches us.

When we embrace the wisdom harvested from the lessons, and blend them with the fruits of fulfillment, that is when we achieve true inner peace. Ultimately I contend this is the highest level of what we seek in this life.

"We can never obtain peace in the outer world until we make peace with ourselves." ~ Dalai Lama XIV

Where Are We Now?

After opening The Jungle Reef Inn, in Roatan, Honduras Leanne, Daeyten, Auka & Miki and myself resided onsite for about seven months. We returned to Canada in May 2017 to care for my father who was suffering from mesothelioma. He passed in August of 2017, after a long, brave fight.

In December of 2017, as we prepared to return to Roatan, I was offered an opportunity to return to a sales management role in the building materials industry which was too good to refuse.

As of the time of publishing, Leanne and I have returned to semi retirement living. Leanne teaches yoga on beaches whenever/wherever possible. I offer coaching and consulting whenever the weather allows. We're always careful to ensure sun and nice weather never goes to waste.

While Auka passed in 2018, Miki continues to enjoy the adventure lifestyle that we've carved out. During summer we enjoy RV living in Canada. When the leaves start to fall its back to sailing south until the butter melts.

It's not a life for everyone, but it's the perfect one for us!

Acknowledgements

The list of people who contributed to me becoming the person that wrote this book is far too long to list here, but I thank every one of you who have been a part of my journey!

Special thanks to my first-year college Business Communication teacher, the late Lynne Woolstencroft. I thank you for the time you invested in me. I came into your class thinking I was a hotshot, who knew it all. You quickly taught me what I didn't know, then you invested the time in teaching what I needed to know. I hope they have bookstores in heaven.

WAYS TO FOLLOW US

If you enjoyed our story and would like to stay in touch with us and our continuing adventures here's how:

- www.facebook.com/WithoutACompassByShawnHamill
- www.shawnhamillconsulting.com
- www.facebook.com/ShawnHamillConsulting
- www.linkedin.com/in/shawnahamill/
- www.facebook.com/TheDoghouseTourCA
- www.facebook.com/TranquilYogaWithLeanne
- www.patreon.com/TheDoghouseTour

Your Opinion Matters – Please Review

Please don't forget to let me, and the rest of the world know what you thought. Leave a review good or bad, on Amazon, or on my book page. Your thoughts matter!

About the Author

Shawn was a sales manager, rising through the ranks of the corporate world and building a reputation as a results-getter in the Home Improvement CPG Space. His sales, relationship and team-building skills, combined with his direct style, opened up a wealth of opportunity in the business world. He was well on his way to financial stability and a good life. It was a safe life that enabled him to be a provider, a husband and a dad, but seemingly constricted his ability to live his best life – a life of purpose, fulfillment.

After traveling extensively to meet the demands of his busy career, he woke up one day to ask, "There's got to be more?" Suddenly, he began to question whether career success was enough? Shawn was living to work, focussed on more – more career success, more financial security, more ability to provide. He discovered that success was a double-edged sword. While every victory in the board room brought an immediate high, it seemed like it pulled him further away from his true self. It left him feeling uninspired and burnt out.

www.ingramcontent.com/pod-product-compliance
Lightning Source LLC
Chambersburg PA
CBHW071451040426
42444CB00008B/1291